# The
# Turning
# POINT

# The Turning Point

"Dr. Prasad, one of the country's most successful and original addiction specialists, has now offered us a road map for kicking stress."

—STEVE KROFT, *60 Minutes* CBS news correspondent

"Dr. Prasad makes a strong case not just for managing stress but for banishing it altogether from your life. I agree completely that any stress is bad stress, no matter what the headlines tell you. This new book will show you that the stress-free life is indeed possible."

—ROBERT EPSTEIN, PhD, former editor-in-chief, *Psychology Today*; author of *The Big Book of Stress Relief Games*

"A highly personal and insightful account of new approaches to conceptualizing stress and its reduction. This book will be of interest to both general readers and professionals focused on stress disorders."

—FRED R. VOLKMAR, MD, Irving B. Harris Professor, Chief of Child Psychiatry at Yale New Haven Hospital

# The Turning POINT

**BALASA PRASAD, MD**

**PREETHAM GRANDHI, MD**

PLAIN SIGHT PUBLISHING

An Imprint of Cedar Fort, Inc.

Springville, Utah

© 2012 Balasa Prasad and Preetham Grandhi

ISBN 13: 978-1-4621-1095-7

Published by Plain Sight Publishing, an imprint of Cedar Fort, Inc.,
2373 W. 700 S., Springville, UT 84663
Distributed by Cedar Fort, Inc. www.cedarfort.com

LIBRARY OF CONGRESS CATALOGING-IN-PUBLICATION DATA
Prasad, Balasa, author.
The turning point : conquering stress with courage, clarity, and confidence / Balasa Prasad, MD.
  pages cm
ISBN 978-1-4621-1095-7 (alk. paper)
1. Stress (Psychology) 2. Stress management. I. Grandhi, Preetham, 1968-, contributor. II. Title.

BF575.S75P735 2012
155.9'042--dc23

2012035032

Cover design by Erica Dixon
Cover design © 2012 by Lyle Mortimer
Edited and typeset by Melissa J. Caldwell

Printed in the United States of America

10  9  8  7  6  5  4  3  2  1

Printed on acid-free paper

## Special thanks

I thank Heidi Bell for her talented editing
and guidance on chapter organization.
—*Balasa Prasad, MD*

I thank the staff of Bronx Children's Psychiatric Center
for their support in my work to guide children and their parents.
—*Preetham Grandhi, MD*

# Contents

# Acknowledgments

Not so long ago, I struggled to dictate ordinary memoranda in my official capacity as head of the department of anesthesia at Mount Vernon Hospital in Mount Vernon, New York. My secretaries had their work cut out for them, editing and redrafting without losing the meaning and the context of my memos. But I have come a long way since then. I am more surprised than anyone to now be writing the preface to my fifth book. My transformation from a clumsy writer into at least a mediocre one with a meaningful message to share did not happen overnight. Apart from a dedicated interest in accomplishing something in my life, I owe this great feat to many people in my life and to Our Maker (Nature).

First of all, I owe a great deal to my mother for being wonderful and caring, and for introducing her four children at a young age to uncompromising moral values. Second, I owe a lot to my father, who taught us the advantages of expressing our values in practical ways every day. Working long hours as a cardiologist, it was difficult for my father to keep in touch with his children and tune in to our daily needs. He addressed this challenge by establishing the cardinal rule in our household that he would spend time with his children every night. While we sometimes had to stay up a couple of hours later and lose a little sleep, our father felt that it was crucial for him to steer us in the right direction from a young age. During our nightly family gatherings, he instilled a sense of courage, confidence, compassion, and common sense in all of us, while simultaneously teaching us to survive the harsh environment and hard times that most of us encounter in life.

He pointed out that we could not hope to bask in the comforts of an easy, happy-go-lucky lifestyle, thinking that karma would resolve our problems. He trained us to withstand stress of any kind and face oncoming challenges without hesitation. He expected us to express our thoughts and ideas freely, on anything from politics to our personal interests, because, he said, thoughts trapped inside the mind are useless unless they are unleashed in a coherent, appealing manner. But he warned us to be prepared for constructive criticism and encouraged us to receive it with an open mind. He would say, "Tough it out. This world is not an easy place to live in." I am convinced to this day that my father's lessons contained the secret to success in life: One can succeed at anything as long as one is operating from a base of discipline, diligence, and dedication.

My beautiful wife and my one-and-only charming, brilliant daughter have also contributed a great deal to this book. My wife has encouraged me at every step and helped to sustain my confidence as I wrote not just this book but my other four books as well. To allow me to concentrate on my writing, she has shielded me from day-to-day frustrations, despite her own busy schedule, which includes managing my office practice, maintaining our house, and authoring her own vegetarian cookbook, *Indian Vegetarian Cooking from an American Kitchen* (Random House, 1998), which adapts nutritious Indian dishes to suit an American lifestyle. For many years she has been the powerhouse in my life. Since her intellectual abilities supersede mine, I can always count on her for a sensible and meaningful interpretation of an issue. She keeps both my daughter and me captivated with her unconditional love and affection. She makes me feel that I am in heaven, not in this imperfect world.

My daughter, in contrast, has acted as my coordinator and cultural critic. She is a busy mother and wife, a part-time manager for a medical billing business, and the author of a flexitarian cookbook, *Spice Up Your Life* (Cedar Fort, 2009). With her help, I have attempted and, I hope, succeeded at bridging the gap between Eastern philosophy and Western lifestyle.

Dr. Preetham Grandhi, my son-in-law, a board-certified adult and pediatric psychiatrist, has assisted me in collecting pertinent clinical data about human habits and behavior. I am grateful for his contributions, especially the chapter on childhood stress. He too is an author of a psychiatric thriller, *A Circle of Souls* (Cedar Fort, 2010).

I am also indebted to my patients, who come to my office with so much trust in my moral judgment and faith in my technical abilities. These patients have driven me to find solutions to their problems and, where no solutions exist, to develop them. It is my patients' appreciation that has encouraged me to stay the course until I could puzzle out the often elusive answers to their dilemmas.

Last but not least, I am ever so grateful to Our Maker (Nature) for giving me the capacity to recognize the hardships that we endure on this earth and the ability to compute some simple solutions to our predicaments.

# Introduction

—————

My intention in writing this book is to guide individuals step-by-step to a life free of stress. I was encouraged to write it by the many patients I have treated with my Turning Point Program, a counseling program designed to conquer stress. I call the program "Turning Point" because it helps to change patients' perspectives on stress and to empower them to turn their lives around.

Rest assured that I will not be boring readers with the same old material on how stress can damage your life and how we all should relax more. Rather, I will open a new dimension so that readers might understand the nature of stress and, in doing so, understand how to conquer it. If we understand that each of us has a role in creating the stress that plagues us, we will have a chance to live stress-free.

I have tried to make this book both as simple and as compelling as possible. However, certain topics remain somewhat technical in spite of my best efforts to simplify them. Even though you may scratch your head at times while reading about these topics, I am sure you will find them fascinating, meaningful, and useful in the end. I'm also certain that, like me and like my patients, you'll find no greater pleasure in life than that which results from thumbing your nose at stress.

Stress spares no one in the world; it is by nature ubiquitous and vicious, knowing no geographical, racial, or economic boundaries. People from other parts of the world may call stress by different names, but they all mean the same thing. If we are going to conquer stress, we must follow the rules of engagement for any battle we intend to win: We must know all about our opponent and his intentions. We must define our goals and decide on a viable plan of action. And we must execute our plan with confidence.

We'll begin by defining the nature and parameters of stress by answering the following questions:

*What is stress?*
*Why is it bad for us?*
*Why must we conquer stress rather than manage it?*
*How can each of us lead a stress-free life?*

## WHAT IS STRESS?

Stress is the emotional discomfort we often feel when things do not go as planned in our lives or a deep mental anguish triggered by adversity. Stress is the nemesis of three elements we all need—peace of mind, good health, and the spirit of freedom. Whether stress results from day-to-day burdens, an addiction, a phobia, conflicts at work or with family members, or the seeming impossibility of reaching a life goal, it stands in the way of living a pleasant, productive, secure, and meaningful life. Severe stress triggered by a life-threatening event or other traumatic situations, such as a parent losing a child, can cause flashbacks that play like a broken record in the mind. I have seen stress, like a termite, eat the body and mind of an individual from the inside out.

## WHY IS STRESS BAD FOR US?

If unchecked, stress incapacitates us and prevents us from reaching our full potential. Psychologically, stress keeps us from taking charge of our destinies by undermining our courage, clarity, and confidence. Physically, stress wreaks havoc on the body. When we are stressed-out, we are more prone to developing

- gastric ulcers, which may turn to cancer
- high blood pressure
- heart problems

2

- breathing problems
- insomnia
- neurological problems, such as headaches, irritable bowel syndrome, and stroke
- diabetes
- immunological problems, such as eczema and psoriasis

In reality, no system of the body can escape the wrath of stress.

## WHY MUST WE CONQUER STRESS RATHER THAN MANAGE IT?

There is a big difference between managing stress and conquering stress. Managing stress means you allow it to continue to exist and learn only how to cope with it when it crops up. That means stress will continue to accompany you everywhere and bother you at every twist and turn of your life. Managing stress uses up time and energy that might be better spent working to reach your goals. Conquering stress, on the other hand, means freeing yourself from it forever, which will allow you to travel light. People who travel light journey far and fast toward their goals. Because stress is generated inside us, if we want to conquer it, we have no choice but to defeat it on its own turf and terms.

FIRST CASE IN POINT: An individual who experiences high levels of stress before and during airline travel might manage this problem by avoiding flying altogether or by taking antianxiety medications (such as Xanax, Valium, or Propranolol), or even by drinking alcohol to calm his nerves before and during a flight. He might also employ relaxation techniques such as breathing exercises or meditation. These measures may appease stress for short periods, but they do not conquer it. In fact, managing this type of stress only guarantees that the individual who fears flying will be held hostage to that fear for the rest of his life. However, an individual who addresses all irrational fears—including the fear of flying—at their root can conquer stress and free himself to pursue his goals without hindrance from any source.

SECOND CASE IN POINT: An unhappy marriage inflicts pain, suffering, and stress on those involved. It takes a toll on their emotional well-being, their physical health, their professional performance, their personal security, and their spirits. Trying to manage this situation by ignoring the facts and opting for temporary relief in the form of anti-depressants, tranquilizers, smoking and alcohol, or cheating on one's spouse will make matters only worse. The only way to conquer stress in this situation is for the couple to face the facts with courage, understand them with clarity, and take appropriate action with confidence.

In my opinion, there are only two choices for an unhappily married couple who wants to lead a stress-free life. Either they identify their differences and resolve them amicably, or they dissolve the marriage and move forward separately. The first option is the best option, especially if children are involved. Happily married couples lead productive, secure, and stress-free lives and provide a wonderful example to their children. I have been happily married for forty-three years. My wife and I are best friends. We support and protect each other without hesitation because we care for, respect, and trust each other—three elements necessary to bind a couple.

A happy marriage calls for a lot of give and take between partners, but give and take doesn't work when someone is keeping score. Partners must give their best unreservedly to the partnership, and when both partners do so, balance and happiness are the result. I believe marriage is an equal partnership and that neither gender nor earning capacity should rule the household. Both parties play an equally important role in keeping the house in order. Truth be told, my wife makes more adjustments to accommodate me than I make for her, and that makes me love her more. Being happily married certainly makes conquering stress in other areas of life much easier. It is no secret that children from happy marriages are physically stronger and mentally more stable than children whose parents are stressed about their marriage.

## HOW CAN EACH OF US LEAD A STRESS-FREE LIFE?

Can an individual truly conquer such a powerful demon as stress? I can tell you, unequivocally, yes! I beat stress at its own game and on its own turf, and if *I* did it, anyone with an ounce of pride can do it as well. I began life in a home run by happily married parents, but even so, it took some time and personal growth for me to get in touch with myself, with my surroundings, and with Nature (Our Maker). Through life's many lessons, I have learned to strive to bring out my best, make the most of my life, and improve the world within my limits.

I know now that my own salvation rests with leading a simple, straightforward, and sanguine life according to the laws of Nature. Nature has given me the gifts of life, health, compassion, and reasonable intelligence, and it dictates that I safeguard and develop these gifts. I will never compromise these principles under any circumstances. When I have to endure hardships, I do so with no regrets. And even the most serious hardships cannot take away the values I will uphold until my last breath. Hitherto, my strategy has served me well: I lead a peaceful, prosperous, productive life.

I have also watched scores of my patients conquer stress using the same method I used. None of us did it, however, with a quick fix or a magic pill. My approach, while simple, is not necessarily easy to implement. You cannot conquer stress by flipping a few chemical switches in the brain. Stress is a problem of the mind, not the brain—the psychological rather than the physical—and our minds have ingrained thought patterns that are often challenging to change.

My method encourages neither optimism nor pessimism but plain realism. For example, we all know that we are not permanent residents of this world but temporary passengers who live for only a short period on this earth. Keeping this fact at the forefront of our minds helps us adjust our priorities and expectations to the realities of life. Realists have the courage and the will to accept the world as it exists. Realists do not have to like the facts of life, but they must have the audacity to face them as they unfold.

My Turning Point Program is based on my own experience and the experiences of my many patients. Using the three-step method summarized below, anyone can conquer stress by systematically adopting a pragmatic outlook and a healthy attitude.

1.  *Set the Stage with Courage*: The process of conquering stress begins with having the courage to face yourself and the world. This process begins with tuning in to the laws of Nature. Understanding Nature will lead you to learn more about yourself—who you really are and what your strengths, weaknesses, talents, and aspirations

are. Understanding Nature will also help you look outward and grasp, with a realist's eye, what this world is all about. For example, this world is a battleground, not a playground.

2. *Devise a Strategy with Clarity*: While none of us has full control over how long we live on this earth, we certainly control how well we lead our lives. In my experience, a successful life strategy focuses on quality rather than quantity. I consider an individual truly successful if the life he has lived leaves a broad smile on his face at the time of departure from this world. With quality of life in mind, I encourage my patients to clearly define their goals and to clearly understand the price they will pay to reach each one. Nothing in life is free, and even peace of mind comes with a price tag. I encourage my patients to differentiate between their needs and wants and to battle wisely to reach their goals. My patients and I carefully craft a suitable strategy to help them navigate through good times and bad times. In India, we believe that good times test one's ability to remain humble and well grounded, whereas bad times test one's skill to survive hardship. There is no end to the testing, because life is a constant process of balancing.

3. *Execute the Strategy with Confidence*: Devising a successful life strategy requires clarity and patience. However, putting a life strategy into action is even more difficult. You must be prepared to persevere without looking back. You must also expect the unexpected and be ready to change your strategy at any given turn if it is not working to help you reach your goals. You must be nimble and savvy. You must always keep your spirits high and remain confident that, one way or another, you will complete whatever task you have set for yourself.

It is important to note that in my private practice I have had patients who have difficulty conquering stress even after learning these concepts. In an office setting, I can guide these patients through the steps of the Turning Point Program and make necessary adjustments to their thought processes and help clarify their life strategies. Additionally, for people who have difficulty executing their life strategies, I offer the option of a powerful Turning Point treatment I have devised using a small dose of methohexital sodium (Brevital sodium). Historically, this medication has been known as a "truth serum" for its ability to induce a state called "twilight sleep," in which patients are relaxed, uninhibited, and talkative, although they might not remember upon waking what they talked about.

The medication helps me to access the part of the patient's mind where primitive emotions, such as fear and rage, reside. These emotions, usually out of sight of our conscious minds, can spur reactions in the present, even though their origins are in the past. We often cannot explain a strong emotional reaction in the present in a rational way because it is triggered by an old emotional experience stored in our unconscious. Methohexital sodium allows me to access the unconscious while at the same time allowing me to access the patient's intellect and instincts. I have found that these treatments help my patients see more clearly what emotions are standing between them and their goals. The treatments also boost patients' confidence and self-esteem, which gives them a head start at successfully executing their life strategies.

In these special sessions, it usually becomes apparent that the patient is being hindered by an irrational fear. While the patient is in a receptive frame of mind, we discuss the fear, its origins, and the plan of action to counter it. I tell the unconscious that it is time for the patient to face repressed, often unpleasant emotions with courage and to behave like a brave and responsible adult rather than a frightened child. These sessions, which usually last between thirty and forty-five minutes, are safe and powerful. It takes a patient about five minutes to awake from a Turning Point Treatment, and he or she is ready to go home fifteen to twenty minutes later.

The chapters that follow illustrate each step of my Turning Point Program in a way that will help you set the stage with courage, devise a life strategy with clarity, and execute the strategy with confidence in order to get the upper hand on your own stress and conquer it once and for all.

*Part I:*

---

# Everyday Stress

---

*One*

---

# The Burden of Stress

Gina was a twenty-eight-year-old patient who came to see me for anxiety and insomnia. I began her treatment, as I do with each of my patients, by asking her to describe what had brought her to my office. How a patient introduces and describes a problem indicates to me the nature of the problem and how to treat it. I learn a lot in those first five minutes, and I learn even more by paying attention to the tone of the consultation, the direction our conversation takes, and the patient's body language.

"God is not listening to my prayers, Dr. Prasad," Gina said. She told me that all her life she'd done God's work. She was a devout Catholic. She and her husband went to Sunday Mass regularly. They had participated in church-sponsored community activities from the day they'd joined the church. Yet Gina said, "I can't help but feel that God has abandoned us in our hour of need. For the first time in my life, I'm lost. I don't know who to turn to for help."

It was apparent that Gina was experiencing acute mental anguish. Was it possible that God had abandoned her? I couldn't speak for God, but I told her not to despair. "There is a solution to every problem," I said, "but many times a person in distress may not be able to see the solution right away."

I was interested to know why Gina felt God had ignored her pleas

11

for help. She told me that she'd grown up in a traditional Catholic family. Her father, a white-collar professional, was the main breadwinner and head of the household, and her mother worked in the home taking care of Gina and her siblings. It was a close-knit nuclear family. Gina respected and trusted both her parents. She was told by them and by her clergy that if she were true to the gospel, to Jesus and the Bible, God would forgive her sins and take care of her forever. As long as she had faith in God, she was led to believe, her problems would be solved by the loving, caring, and forgiving Almighty. As an adult, Gina still believed from the bottom of her heart that God would take good care of her just as her parents and then her husband had done.

Gina's husband, Tom, was a handsome and charming young man when she met him during her senior year of high school. By her account, it was love at first sight. After high school, Gina went to college, and Tom pursued a career in construction. After they were married, Tom joined a construction company as a carpenter and then started his own home-remodeling business. Gina graduated from college and joined a law firm as an office manager. At age twenty-three, when she got pregnant with her first child, she gave up her job, assuming the traditional role of a housewife. Tom was a hard worker and good provider. By the time Gina came to see me, she was twenty-eight years old and had two daughters, ages five and three.

A year before she visited me, Gina's life was cruising along on autopilot until Tom had a hunting accident. Tom enjoyed hunting with his friends as a way of relaxing and recharging his battery. But while pursuing an animal in the woods, he fell and severely injured his back. While his injury was a definite hardship, Gina assumed that Tom would recover within a short time and that their lives would return to normal. She did not anticipate the possibility that even after six months, Tom would be virtually crippled by pain and back spasms and unable to do any physically demanding construction work.

Because this accident was neither work related nor anybody's fault, Tom was not entitled to any kind of compensation from any source. A few months later, he lost his health insurance because he was unable to pay the premiums. The money they had saved could stretch for one year but left them unable to pay their home mortgage payments. The final blow to Gina's ego and confidence came when they were turned down by welfare agencies because they still had some equity in their house.

As these events unfolded, Gina continued to believe that God would not let her family down. She prayed for a miracle from heaven. But as time went by, Tom did not get better, and the anticipated miracle did not happen. Gina began to lose faith in God. She felt angry at God and betrayed by Him, which in turn caused her to feel guilty. Believing in God and being a part of the church had always been a security blanket for her. The fact that God wasn't taking care of her now, wasn't answering her prayers after caring for her so well all her life, only added to her feelings of insecurity over what the future might hold.

For the first time in her life, Gina felt stress in the form of anxiety and difficulty sleeping. She went to her physician, who prescribed antidepressants, sleep aids, and tranquilizers to manage the stress. The medications temporarily helped her to sleep better and numbed her emotional pain. But then she began to experience nightmares, which would wake her up in the middle of the night with cold sweats, heart palpitations, and shortness of breath. The entire family was engulfed in stress. Even her five- and three-year-old daughters became agitated and cranky and got into fights with their friends at school. Gina was frantic and needed a practical solution to prevent her family from imploding.

Gina finished telling her story and said that a friend had recommended me. She looked at me expectantly, and I could see that she had pinned all her hopes on me to somehow reverse her misfortunes. I leaned forward and looked directly into Gina's eyes. I asked her if she was ready to hear the truth and nothing but the truth about her situation as I saw it. Gina was startled at first, but after a few seconds she had regained her composure and was ready to hear what I had to say.

"You are mistaken when you say that God is not listening to your prayers," I began. "In actuality it is you who are not listening. You have turned a deaf ear to God's directives. If you were listening to God, you would stop feeling sorry for yourself and looking for an easy way out. Because of an unforeseen and an unexpected incident, your life has been turned upside down. Your husband can no longer be the bread-winner of your family. However, you are bright, educated, talented, and in good health. It is time for you to take charge of the family and be the breadwinner. Let your husband take care of the children until he finds a suitable job."

Gina sat across from me with a stunned look on her face.

"You and Tom have developed an excellent network in your church," I continued. "Ask for help. Tell your fellow parishioners point-blank that you are not looking for handouts. You are ready to work during the day and go school at night if necessary to develop any new skills that you need to survive. You are asking them to help you find a job if they can." I reminded her that church is not just a place of worship. It is a symbol of self-actualization, inspiration, and hope. It is a place congregants team up and pool their resources and talents to help each other in times of need.

Gina had made a passing comment that she was good at flower arrangement. I suggested that in addition to a full-time job, she seek some part-time work at a nearby florist. I also suggested that every Sunday in church she exhibit flower arrangements for sale and inform fellow churchgoers, family members, and friends that she was willing to provide flowers for any occasion. She could split any profits made through selling flowers in church with the church. I also suggested that Tom take some computer courses. Maybe he could work from home through the Internet.

I told Gina to, with her physician's guidance, stop taking all the medications she had been prescribed for stress. In my experience, such medications only dull the senses and cloud the judgment. Medications have never motivated an individual to take charge of her destiny. I told Gina that she would need to be cool, calm, calculating, and courageous if she wanted to beat the stress and lead a pleasant, productive life again.

Gina sat in silence for a few seconds after I stopped talking. Then she said, "So you're telling me that I'm not listening to God."

"Yes," I said. "Gina, you asked God for a miracle without realizing that the miracle is you. You have the ability to rescue your family. The day you recognize this fact and are willing to do whatever it takes within the confines of the laws of Nature to put your family back on track, you will conquer the stress and control not only your destiny but also your family's destiny as well."

Gina perked up. She was beginning to realize that while she was in a difficult situation, she was certainly not helpless to pull herself out of it. She thanked me for my advice and promised me that she would listen to God without fail.

Fortunately for Gina, the Turning Point Program provided the ammunition she needed to take charge of her life. She did not need my Turning Point Treatments to execute her plan of action. She called me a year later to tell me that she had been working outside the home for some time and was happy about it. She was sleeping well and coping with life's ups and downs without any medications. She was, in other words, truly at peace with herself. Tom had also secured a decent job as a computer programmer. I congratulated Gina on a job well done and assured her that she would never feel helpless again for the rest of her life.

Gina's ordeal raises some pertinent questions.

1. Why didn't she and Tom come up with solutions to their problems by themselves?
2. Why didn't family members and friends come to their rescue when they were in deep financial trouble?
3. Why didn't the doctor who prescribed medications for Gina's anxieties and insomnia guide her properly?

Gina and Tom were caught off guard by his accident. Never having dealt with such serious personal problems before, they were in a state of shock. They were also ashamed to fully disclose their financial situation to their families or fellow parishioners. Tom was frightened by his physical disability. He was preoccupied with his injured back and his feelings of helplessness, which prevented him from seeking a solution to his and Gina's problems. For her part, Gina was locked into her blind religious faith and preoccupied with the idea that God should magically, without any effort on her part, deliver her and her family from their hardships. The doctor who prescribed medications for Gina was probably not qualified to deal with her psychological situation. Many medical doctors are uncomfortable addressing their patients' psychological and emotional issues. Maybe he recommended that Gina see a mental health specialist and she failed to follow his advice.

It is not easy to predict how a stressed-out individual will react to an adverse situation, but most people become so focused on the problem at hand that it becomes the whole world, with no room for solutions. Through her work with me, Gina gained the courage to shift her perspective away from what she couldn't do to what she could do, thereby setting the stage for her battle against the stress in her life. Only then was she able to acknowledge the skills and strengths she had previously ignored because of her assumptions about how God's work would manifest in her life. Recognizing the skills and strengths Nature had given her led Gina to devise a plan to rid her life of stress for good.

Gina and Tom's experience with such an intense level of stress put both of them on guard for the rest of their lives. The process of finding and implementing solutions to their problems helped them realize that they are mentally, emotionally, and spiritually strong enough to tackle any kind of situation that might arise in the future. This knowledge and confidence has made them the masters of their destiny. They have conquered stress once and for all.

To overpower stress, one must first grasp its nature. Stress feeds on feelings of hopelessness, fear, and anger. It thrives in the realm of the irrational. Its natural enemies, therefore, are hope, rational thinking, and innovation. Since no two individuals are exactly alike, no two people will respond the same way to the same stimulus. What is stressful to one person—a small enclosed space (claustrophobia), for instance—might not even register with another. Two people can share a fear of flying, but the origins of their fear are as individual as their fingerprints. For some people, the heightened anxieties and restlessness associated with acute stress, as in a phobia, can feel strangely comforting, like a security blanket.

There are four general areas of stimulus that create stress in most of us. The first is the death of a loved one. The second is the feeling of insecurity. The third is the failure to reach a goal. And the fourth is rejection. A feeling of stress in turn often triggers fear. A little fear is not always a bad thing, as it encourages us to be cautious. But a heightened sense of fear can eclipse our courage, clarity, and confidence and make it seem impossible to resolve the issue at hand. Some of us respond to our feelings of fear with anger ("I'm an idiot for fearing something so silly!"), shame ("Why can't I be a more courageous person?"), or self-pity ("Why is this happening to me?"). I've often seen this type of cascading response in phobias, such as fear of heights, elevators, highways, darkness, tunnels, and flying, or in cases of performance anxiety, such as stage fright, fear of public speaking, fear of failure, and impotence.

In the stress dynamic, an individual is on one side, and the uncomfortable, unbearable, and frightening situation or circumstance is on the other. These forces are never equal; one is always poised to overpower the other. So how do we keep a situation from triggering a stress response so that we might emerge victorious? The answer is simple, although implementing it is not: we choose either to change the situation or to reframe it so that it is no longer stressful to us. The most desirable way to resolve this impasse is to change the situation to our liking and to our advantage. But this option is often either difficult or impossible to implement, since many things in this world are out of our control. The other option, if one wants to live stress-free, is to accept and adjust to the situation. This second option is relatively straightforward on its face, but it is hard for most of us to accept on an emotional level.

While I was writing this chapter, an article in the *New York Times* caught my attention.[1] I was disheartened to read that the emotional health of college freshmen in the United States is at its lowest level since researchers began collecting data twenty-five years ago. Students are more depressed and are experiencing higher levels of stress, and many of them are coping with these problems by using medications such as antidepressants and tranquilizers.

The root of the problem, according to the article, is cultural: First, a downturn in the US economy, which has led to high unemployment and a record budget deficit, has caused a substantial reduction in college grants from the government and endowments from the private sector. As a result, fewer students are able to procure financial aid other than student loans. Second, many parents, due to unemployment or underemployment, are unable to help their children pay their tuition as they might once have. Students themselves are having increasing difficulty finding part-time jobs to help finance their educations. College students today are unsure that after graduation they will even be able to secure decent jobs with good salaries, and they know they will graduate with the added pressure of large student loans. Most of them are convinced that they will never be better off than their parents, no matter how hard they work.

What is the solution for college students struggling under the burden of stress? As I mentioned, the first option is to change the stressful situation to their advantage, but in this case that would mean reversing the tide of the economic downturn. As college students have little control over major economic factors, it's unlikely they can do much to change the situation. The better option is to accept and adjust to the situation. If a student determines after diligent investigation that loans are the only way to afford college, then that student can either choose to borrow the money or choose a different route than college. This choice must be made with a clear understanding of the price to be paid either way. Large loans mean sacrifice after graduation, whether that means, for example, taking a lower-paying job that isn't your first choice or going without a car for a few years. Choosing not to go to college means working hard to obtain career training in other ways, whether through apprenticeships, unpaid internships, or working one's way up the ladder in a chosen profession.

In any case, young people considering college and careers must be encouraged to look at the big picture. When they do, they will see endless opportunities. A changing job market, for example, means new job opportunities for those who recognize the trends and position themselves advantageously. The world has changed a great deal since their parents grew up, went to college, and were virtually guaranteed well-paying jobs. But rather than dwell on the ways that the world has changed to their disadvantage, these young people must open their eyes and look at the world as it is and has always been—a challenging place where nothing is gained without a great deal of effort. They must define their goals according to the gifts Nature has given them and then go after their goals with confidence and perseverance.

I'm currently treating a young, bright but socially awkward individual who is unable to find a job as a librarian after recently completing his masters in library science. He chose this field because it requires minimal social interaction while fostering his love for books. Unfortunately, advances in technology and reduced funding at the state and local levels have eliminated the need for more librarians. Thus, his efforts to find a position in this field are futile.

He is also a sensitive, insecure, and anxious individual. He is not the adventurous type and frets changes in life. Being young, unemployed, and dependent on his parents has stressed him out. I told him if the opportunities are unavailable in his field and hometown, he must reinvent himself. He has to expand his search into other fields that may take him out of state or even out of the country. For example, his strong command over the English language qualifies him to teach English. There are many developing countries like China that are searching for good English teachers. He must seek out any and all opportunities, because opportunities will not come looking for him. I convinced him that if I can do it, he could do it too. When I graduated from medical school in India and landed a residency in England, I was scared to leave India. However, in pursuit of a better and brighter future, I took a bold step, and it has paid off. He liked the example of my own experience and took my comments to heart. After two Turning Point Treatments, with courage and confidence, he has started to apply for jobs all over the world.

Now that I've described in detail the two options we all have when facing stressful situations, you might be thinking that you can craft a third option, one that is more convenient or appealing than the other two. But I'll warn you now that Nature dictates only the two options I've already described. The third option is a false option, one that originates from an unwillingness to look honestly and rationally at one's life. Choosing the hypothetical third option makes it possible only to manage stress, not conquer it. We all must choose either option one or option two at every step, every twist, and every turn of our lives.

Let us analyze a smoking habit as an example. A smoker has become concerned about his health, and as a result, smoking has begun to cause him stress. To rid his life of this stress, he has two options: One, he might choose to be a comfortable smoker by accepting both the pleasures and the health problems that go hand-in-hand with the habit. Or two, he might choose to be a comfortable nonsmoker by accepting that he must sacrifice the pleasure of smoking to avoid the health problems that result from the habit.

Let us say that a particular smoker tries to quit smoking but fails. His stress increases because he failed to reach the goal he set for himself. He argues that giving up cigarettes is impossible because he is so addicted. He decides that there is a third option: He will smoke in a more healthy way—he will buy cigarettes with lower tar content. He will reduce the number of cigarettes he smokes daily. When he feels he is smoking to excess, he will use nicotine patches and gum. He will take vitamins and other nutritional supplements to bolster his health. He thinks that somehow this intricate system will allow him to have it both ways, to have the pleasure of smoking without the health costs. But in the end, he knows he is lying to himself, and he still feels miserable about smoking. Stress is still dictating his actions, because he is managing it rather than conquering it.

If this smoker were able to set aside his stress-related fear, anger, and hopelessness and view the situation rationally and honestly, he might see that he continues to smoke not because he *cannot* quit but because he does not *want* to quit. The bottom line is that he enjoys smoking and does not wish to sacrifice the pleasure it brings him. But at the same time, he is not happy about the impact smoking has on his health. The tension in the situation (stress) comes from his refusal to take responsibility for his decision, whether that decision is to smoke or not to smoke. By choosing option one or option two, he will automatically take responsibility for his actions, and his stress will evaporate.

However, when choosing between option one and option two, it is always to our advantage to work with Nature rather than against it. For example, if the smoker decides to be a comfortable nonsmoker, as Nature intends, he frees himself from stress while simultaneously enjoying good health. However, if he chooses to be a comfortable smoker and accepts the consequences, he will be free from stress but not from the ill effects of smoking. Similarly, an obese person who wishes to live stress-free must decide to either eat as she pleases and accept the consequences or pay attention to what, when, where, and how much she eats for the rest of her life and develop an exercise routine to stay fit, healthy, and energetic. If such a person opts for the false third option, she might categorize her weight problem as a sickness and try diet aids, fat farms, and fad diets to "cure" it. Such approaches will take her nowhere and will certainly not conquer the stress she feels about her weight. Such an individual will remain both obese and unhappy about it until she looks at her choices honestly and rationally and takes responsibility for them.

The way you approach the difficulties in your life is up to you. You can choose to manage your stress rather than understand and conquer it. But be warned: If you refuse to analyze the nature of your stress, you will run in circles forever trying to manage it. If you consider vanquishing stress a chore rather than a challenge, the stress will bear down on you and sap your energy until you cave in and allow it to rule your life. The choice is yours.

A CASE IN POINT: John, a forty-one-year-old small-business owner, came to see me because he wanted to conquer his fear of flying and improve his golf game. He had been happily married for twelve years and had two sons aged ten and seven. He had built a successful business from scratch and considered himself a hardworking, honorable individual. With the exception of his fear of flying and his inability to enjoy a relaxed game of golf, he felt his life was complete. Flying and playing golf left him exhausted. He would fret for days about an upcoming flight or golf date. He would be anxious even before boarding a plane and felt panicked most of the time during the flight. If it was a long flight, he would need a couple of days to recover afterward. He usually played golf with business acquaintances, with whom he would often discuss business deals while relaxing in the clubhouse after the game. The first few holes he usually played well, but as he neared the last few holes, he would tense up and make inconceivable mistakes that brought his scores down.

For the past ten years, John had tried to resolve both these issues and had failed. At the time he came to see me, he followed a ritual of taking tranquilizers two to three hours before a flight and then drinking a little alcohol and sometimes taking beta-blockers to stay calm throughout the flight. He followed almost the same routine before a golf game, without the beta-blockers. Lately, his anxiety had worsened and begun affecting other areas of his life. He'd had to increase the amount of medication to get the same level of relief, but the increased dosage affected his clarity and composure. His wife pointed out that he had become irritable and cranky at home and that he snapped at the children more than ever before. John loved his family and did not want them to hate him or fear him.

Once I'd heard John's story, I asked him why, if he was happy with his life but for these two problems, he didn't stay away from flying and golf and move on with his life. John told me that at one point he had asked himself the same question, but he had come to the conclusion that he could not live with the decision to take the coward's way out. He had never turned away from a challenge in his life, and he was not ready to set a precedent. Besides, both flying and playing golf were integral parts of his business. He had to fly to promote and market his products. Treating clients to a game of golf was a way to entertain them, show his appreciation, and develop a powerful network for his business. Certainly, John was in a tough spot.

I wanted to know a little bit more about John's childhood. He told me he came from a blue-collar family. Both his parents had had to work long hours. At times he'd heard them discussing their financial hardships. The way he described himself as a child, I could see that John had always been a proud, sensitive, sentimental, insecure individual. When he was eleven years old, he heard the father of a classmate had died in an auto accident. For several months afterward, John had nightmares about his parents' safety.

In fact, John's fear of flying and playing a poor game of golf were just symptoms, but of what? I told John that his pride and his insecurities had prompted him to work hard and build a successful business to his satisfaction. However, once he had built a good life, instead of enjoying his successes, his insecurities and pride were demanding an absolute assurance from him that he would remain successful and keep his family safe forever. "Every time you board a plane," I told him, "you feel that your family's security is threatened, since you might not land safely. Every time you play golf, you feel your business will be threatened if you don't win. In order to conquer your fears and enjoy peace of mind, you'll have to make a fundamental change in your mind-set. You'll have to give up your insecurities and tone down your pride."

John's insecurities conjured up visions of his death or the loss of his wealth and the toll these things would take on his family. Flying triggered in him the deep-seated fear of death. Playing golf triggered his fear of poverty. These primal fears convinced him that in an instant he could lose it all—his life, his business, the respect of his peers—and robbed him of his courage, clarity, and confidence. I told him that if he wanted to fly comfortably and enjoy a game of golf, he must first conquer the irrational fears at the root of his problems.

John agreed with my analysis and was willing to work with me to vanquish his stress forever. I reminded him that no one in the world knows what the future holds. Therefore, logic dictates that a person can only control his actions, not the results. The sooner John accepted this concept, I told him, the faster his stress would disappear. A healthy dose of fear and insecurity energizes us and spurs us to reach our goals. However, the combination of overactive pride and insecurity dampens our spirit, courage, and confidence and may even prevent us from taking appropriate actions to reach our goals.

I advised John to take appropriate actions regarding airline travel and golf and let Nature take its course. Regarding flying, John could control only his own actions. He could, for example, select an airline with a good track record for safety and make sure weather patterns were relatively conducive to flying. Other conditions he would simply have to accept. He would have to accept that there would be an element of danger in any activity he undertook. Similarly, if he was afraid that his death might cause financial hardship to his family, he could keep his finances in order and take out an adequate, affordable life insurance policy to protect his family. He would also have to mentally disconnect his golf game from his business. He would have to stop playing to impress his clients or his buddies and just enjoy the camaraderie of the game. If he wanted to compete, he would have to compete against his own personal best, with the understanding that winning the hearts and minds of his colleagues rested on how well he enjoyed the game rather than the numbers on the scorecard.

After the consultation, John chose to use my Turning Point Treatments to get a head start in his endeavor. During the treatments, I encouraged him to work with the laws of Nature. He promised to do the best he could with honorable intentions and face the results with courage. Six months later he reported to me that he was able to fly with minimum discomfort. In fact, since his first Turning Point Treatment, he had never panicked during a flight, even without using drugs or alcohol to numb his fear. Nowadays he does not even carry any medications with him when he flies. And he is truly enjoying the game of golf for the first time. His handicap has come down from 110 to 90.

*Two*

---

# The Origins of Stress

Naturally, we would all love to live in a perfect and peaceful world. Unfortunately, such a world does not exist. At a deep level, we all know that our security and survival, our happiness and peace of mind, are not guaranteed. Whenever we feel tested or threatened, we experience stress. Any kind of threat—internal or external, implied or imminent, real or perceived—triggers stress. This is an uncontested fact of life.

All of us face two types of threats constantly: external and internal. External threats originate in the outside environment. We face external threats each day by simply getting out of bed. Every action and transaction we undertake carries with it some kind of danger. The possibility of a terrorist attack is an example of an external threat, as is the threat of layoff in an economic downturn, the chance that a drunken driver will run over an innocent pedestrian, and the risk of betrayal by a trusted friend. Conversely, internal threats originate in either the body or the mind in the form of physical diseases such as cancer, diabetes, and heart disease or psychological problems such as insecurity, addictions, and phobias.

All external threats fall into two broad categories, implied and imminent. For example, statistically speaking, there is an implied external threat associated with getting into a bathtub, where many household accidents take place. But just because bathing carries the risk of injury does not mean we stop bathing. Instead, we install tub liners and safety railings, thereby preventing a majority of accidents and keeping an external implied threat from becoming an imminent one. Even a vehicle operated by a sensible defensive driver carries an external implied threat, because the brakes may fail or the car may skid. A vehicle operated by a reckless driver, on the other hand, is an external imminent threat, meaning that an accident involving the vehicle is bound to happen at some point. A teenage girl who consorts with a stranger via the Internet is ignoring the external implied threat in their interactions. When she agrees to meet the individual in person, the threat to her safety becomes imminent. If we are aware of an implied threat and are proactive against it, we can easily thwart the imminent threat with which it is associated.

I would argue that people are hurt far more often by internal threats than by external threats. Some internal threats, such as cancer, are dictated by Nature, and we have little control over them; they could happen to any one of us. However, addictions—which I consider cancer of the mind—are self-inflicted internal threats. Other internal threats are more slippery. They include arrogance, impatience, over-confidence, greed, and lust. Given a free hand, these characteristics will turn an individual into his own worst enemy and a menace to others. Everyday life is filled with both external and internal threats to our peace of mind. Couples and individuals without children might feel threatened by their own ambitions, unrealistic expectations at work, the needs of aging parents, and the rising cost of living. Couples also have to cope with the threats associated with intimacy, including conflicting goals and unrealistic expectations.

Couples and single people with children understand that parenting is both the most joyous and the most challenging undertaking one can hope to experience. As a father, I can tell you it bestowed upon me a sense of purpose, lifted my spirits after a tough day at work, and gave me an excuse to watch Bugs Bunny or play hide-and-seek with my daughter. Sharing a hug with her every night before bedtime made me feel that all was right with the world. On the flip side, parenthood is rife with external threats to peace of mind in the form of school issues, discipline problems, bullying, and drug or alcohol abuse. Internal threats that create parental stress include illness and unrealistic expectations.

Parental stress is greater for single parents than for couples. Single parenting is more common today than ever before, with one out of every four American children living in a single-parent home.[1] In my experience, single parents feel a high proportion of internal threats; they often feel mentally overwhelmed, frustrated, anxious, and guilty as they try to balance the many facets of family, professional, and personal life. External threats to peace of mind might include a demanding boss, difficult coworkers, too much work with minimal resources, an exhausting commute, kids' extracurricular activities, getting dinner on the table, helping with homework or social problems, finding quality time to spend with the kids, caring for an elderly parent, doing laundry, going grocery shopping, keeping the house in order, and managing the budget.

So how do we cope with these innumerable and perpetual threats to our peace of mind? We can't make them go away, and we can't control them all. First, we have to learn to focus on the threats that we can protect against and let the others fall off the radar. The laws of Nature dictate that we must neutralize internal threats before we can vanquish external threats. Like cancer and addiction, other internal threats, such as arrogance and greed, sap physical strength, dampen the spirit, and cloud the mind. It is crucial we assess and protect ourselves against the internal threats that are within our control and accept the ones that are out of our control. The bad news is that arrogance, impatience, and greed are an integral part of all of our identities, so we cannot eliminate them. The good news is that it is possible to mitigate their influence during our decision-making process. The following chapters explore in greater detail how to recognize, assess, and protect against such internal threats.

The most important aspect of coping with threats is to tackle them head-on rather than to run and try to hide from them. When we face the external and internal threats to our happiness, we gain a powerful head start in our battle to conquer stress. Courage, clarity, and confidence are our three knights in shining armor in this battle. Those of us who live stress-free take each threat as it comes. We analyze its true nature, trace it to its source, and come up with a clear and appropriate strategy to vanquish it.

Parents can vanquish many threats by setting realistic goals and doing their best with the resources at hand. Stress-free parents don't feel guilty about not having enough money or time for their kids, and they don't try to keep up with the Joneses. By refusing to engage with the internal threat of guilt, you can vanquish it as a source of stress. If you live according to your priorities to the best of your ability, there is no need to feel guilty. A plethora of parenting magazines, parenting experts, and tiger moms will tell you how to feel inadequate, but the better option is to trust your own instincts. Kids want little more than your unconditional love and to know that you are there for them when they need you. Spending quality family time might be as simple as playing board games or taking a stroll in the park together. Have a few priorities, and let the rest go. Parents do themselves and their families a favor when they resist the temptation to overextend themselves and their kids, which only creates additional stress.

I advised my patient Gina to seek support from her fellow congregants at church, and I encourage parents in a similar vein to find innovative ways to meet the demands of parenthood. First, children can be trained from a young age to be self-reliant. Consider parenthood in the wild: Bald eagles on their perches in North Dakota, polar bears in the Arctic, and penguins in Antarctica teach their young ones to fend for themselves from the minute they are born. The very survival of these species depends on this strategy, which I call "True Love." Even young children can help at home with age-appropriate household chores such as sorting laundry, setting the table, and loading the dishwasher. By delegating such tasks, parents engender a sense of responsibility in their children and reduce their own workload. I also advise parents to be both organized—for instance to have a large family calendar where appointments and meetings are written—and prepared for the unexpected. Create a reliable support system of family members, friends, and other families who can help you when you need it. For example, single parents might form a co-op to provide child care on a weekly basis. Two parents might get together to take care of the children of four single parents while the other two parents take the time to run errands, keep appointments, attend social events, or just have some time alone at home.

Parents and other busy individuals often find their personal development threatened by time constraints. On a personal level, Nature obligates us to take care of ourselves by eating right, getting adequate sleep, and exercising for thirty minutes each day. When one of my patients complained that she had no time to work out, I suggested that she use her lunch break at work to eat a quick lunch and take a long walk. Nature does not accept our excuses and explanations for our failure to obey its laws. Similarly, I encourage people who feel overwhelmingly busy to disengage from the technologies that allow us to be "connected" twenty-four hours a day, seven days a week. Connecting to work or even to social networking sites can become a compulsion and thus a threat to a balanced, stress-free life.

On the professional front, threats to job security in today's economic climate must be taken seriously, but no job is worth compromising one's principles. It's a good idea to check frequently with your boss to make sure that you understand and are meeting expectations. If you have a family, you might have a frank conversation with your boss and present a plan of action that details how you'll get your job done even if sometimes you have to leave work early. Thanks to current technology, telecommuting is an option for many professionals nowadays. If the threat you feel regarding your job is internal, meaning you feel stressed about work because it doesn't utilize the gifts Nature has given you, keep your eyes and ears open and network for more suitable opportunities.

Some threats, internal and external, originate in our imaginations and so are perceived rather than real. It is sometimes quite difficult to differentiate between an imaginary threat and a legitimate one. Human beings have vivid imaginations, and in that realm, anything is possible. Using such a unique and powerful gift wisely can serve the human race, but using it foolishly can seriously hurt us. Imaginary threats can even push us over the brink into insanity. Hypochondriacs, for example, fret over their physical health so obsessively that they end up living in the shadow of death and disease. An entrenched hypochondriac subjects his body to unnecessary diagnostic tests, medications, and even surgical procedures in search of the mysterious causes of his many symptoms. He learns how to persuade health care professionals to order more medications and treatments so he can put his mind at ease, when none of these things will in fact bring him any peace of mind. Hypochondriacs find a sort of sick solace in misery.

One of my patients who suffered from hypochondria did respond well to the Turning Point Treatments. However, when I was about to pat myself on the back for a job well done, she called to tell me that she was still stressed out, because she now had no health issues to worry about. What would she do with all the time she had on her hands? It took a few months for her to redefine her priorities and channel her energy into more rewarding and productive activities.

Another patient, Harold, came to me after having become obsessed with his blood pressure. He was a fifty-two-year-old man who was meticulous, well organized, responsible, and somewhat insecure. He was also an uptight, impatient perfectionist, disenchanted because the world in which he lived was fraught with hassles and hazards. His stress manifested in the form of anxiety and depression, and he had been taking Xanax, Klonopin, and Zoloft for three years to manage these problems. He worked hard to stay physically fit, and he went to his doctor every six months for a physical. During his last checkup, his doctor had noted that his blood pressure was high and prescribed some medication to bring it down.

The fact that his body was imperfect did not resonate well with Harold. He bought a blood-pressure measuring device and checked his pressure four to five times a day. The more he tried to control it, the more unstable it became. Over the course of one day, his blood pressure would swing from high to low. His doctor told him to calm down and let the medication do its job. But the patient could not put a lid on his obsession. Finally, he came to see me to help solve his problem.

I knew that I had to convince Harold to accept the fact that we live in an imperfect world and that he must work within it willingly as it exists. If I could not help him accept this, he would be stressed-out for the rest of his life and certainly unable to resolve his blood pressure problems. I told him that he had only two choices as dictated by Nature. Either he could change the world to his liking, or he could change himself to adjust to the world. He agreed with me that the first option was impossible. He also agreed that if he did not adjust to the world as it exists, he would be doomed to a life of stress. He agreed to have Turning Point Treatments to help him adjust.

Over the course of three months, I gave him three treatments. One month after the final treatment, he called to tell me that his blood pressure was much more stable than it had been before he came to see me. Noting the positive response of his blood pressure to the changes in his attitude, his doctor had decreased the dose of his medication. Two months after his last Turning Point Treatment, he was able to stop taking Klonopin for anxiety. Four months after his last treatment, he stopped taking Zoloft for depression. Six months after his last treatment, Harold no longer needed any medications at all.

In a letter I received from him, he wrote, *It has now been five months since my final treatment. I am happy to say that I am over the fears I had with health issues, especially those concerning blood pressure. While the issues may not have changed, my outlook has. The fears and the concerns are gone. Whatever comes up I see in perspective and deal with it rationally. I cannot believe the way I was and how difficult I made everything. The best part is that as I gained confidence, my self-esteem improved, and I now have fewer problems. This attitude affects all facets of my life. From family and friends to anything else I do, I am more relaxed and enjoy life more. Every day I thank you for what you did for me.*

The beauty of this case is that, as Harold gained confidence, he saw no need to medicate himself. He stopped allowing his overactive imagination to rule his life and decided to live in the real world.

The power of imagination can be an asset, but, as with hypochondria, it can also be a liability. Since the beginning of recorded history, humans have told imaginative tales of ghosts, goblins, vampires, zombies, and other mythical creatures. While there is no clear scientific evidence to support the existence of such creatures, they have been characterized by many people as an imminent threat and thus have caused immense stress.

A CASE IN POINT: I have personally experienced the feeling of imminent threat from ghosts. Until I was nine years old, my family and I lived in a hundred-year-old colonial house in India. When I was seven, one of my mother's sisters visited us there. None of us knew when she arrived that it would be the last time she would visit us in that house. Of all my maternal aunts and uncles, she was my favorite. She often came for short visits. She was young—twenty-two at the time of her last visit—and a very caring and loving person. Whenever possible, she played cricket in our backyard with me and my friends. She always made a mental note about the things my siblings and I wanted and surprised us with gifts during her visits. A visit from her was a special treat for all of us.

It was a chilly January night. I came home about eight in the evening, tired after playing with my friends for several hours at a nearby playground. My mother forced me to have a hot bath because I was covered in dirt from head to toe. After my bath, I drank a tall glass of warm milk and went to bed. The moment my head rested on my soft pillow, I drifted to sleep. Around 2:00 a.m., a scream from the adjacent bedroom awakened me. In a split second, I jumped out of bed. The house was now silent. Had the scream been real or a nightmare? My aunt slept in the room next to mine. Had something happened to her? My own room was dark, and I was scared and disoriented. I slid back under the covers, where I felt safe. My younger brother, who was five and slept next to me, started to cry. He stretched out his arms, searching for me. I got out of the bed and turned on the lights. While I was consoling him, my two older sisters, who slept in the bedroom across the hall, came running into our room to make sure that we were okay. Once I saw my sisters, I calmed down. By then I heard my mother's voice in the next room. Now all four of us were curious to know what had happened to our aunt.

My eldest sister, who is four years older than me, advised us to stay in the room while she went to investigate. But the three of us could not stay by ourselves, and we followed her into the hallway. The door to our aunt's room was open, and we peeked inside. I saw my aunt sitting on the bed with wide eyes. She held her trembling hands protectively over her neck as she gasped for air. I could clearly see that she was frightened, and I knew that something bad had happened to her. My mother sat on the bed trying to console her. Then my mother noticed that we were standing by the door watching. Immediately she bolted toward us and whispered something into my sister's ear. My sister escorted us back to her room while my mother went back into my aunt's room and closed the door. My sister told us to sleep in her room for the remainder of the night. I asked her what had happened to our aunt, but she shushed me and said she would explain it to me in the morning. I had trouble falling asleep because I couldn't shake the terrified image of my aunt from my head. Eventually I dozed off.

When I woke up, it was seven in the morning. My sisters and brother and I got ready to go to school. Before I left, I went to my aunt's room, curious as to how she was doing. The door was closed, and I leaned against it, listening for any sounds. There was only silence. When I asked my mother about my aunt, she assured me that my aunt was fine and resting. She told us not to disturb her. It was 4:00 p.m. when I came back from school. The first thing I did was go to my aunt's room. The door was open, and my aunt was not there. I looked around the room and noticed that her suitcases were gone. I ran to my mother and wanted to know where my aunt had gone. My mother gave me a cool drink, and while I was sipping it, she told me that my aunt had gotten an emergency telegram requesting that she return home immediately. This explained her absence, but the incident of the previous night remained a mystery. Looking at my worried face, my mother assured me that my aunt was fine and would visit us again as soon as possible. I felt relieved. Even though I took my mother's word for what it was worth, I knew my mother was holding back the truth about her sister.

After that episode, our parents moved a second bed into my sisters' room, and my brother and I slept there for the next two years. During that time, at my mother's insistence, my father had a new house constructed for us. As soon as the new house was ready, we moved in. In the new house, two bedrooms were adjacent to each other with a large sliding door in between. My brother and I slept in one room, while my sisters slept in the other room. The sliding door was always open at night. I liked the idea of having an opening between the two rooms, because I could see my sisters whenever I woke in the middle of the night, and I knew they would be there if I had a nightmare.

Two months after we moved into the new house, I was going to the kitchen for a snack, and I overheard my oldest sister and my mother talking about my aunt. Naturally, I was curious, and I decided to eavesdrop on their conversation. My mother was telling my sister that my aunt was planning to visit us, implying that her sister could come now that we lived in our new house. My mother then told my sister that our old house was haunted. When we first moved into that house, when I was just a baby, one of our neighbors shared a secret about the house with my mother. The neighbor said that a few years before, a twenty-three-year-old pregnant woman had committed suicide in that house. She had come back as a ghost and resided in the house since her death. My mother then saw this ghost, a young woman in a white sari, wandering the halls of our house at night. At first she was startled but not surprised. The second time, she spoke with the ghost and made a secret pact with her. My mother had no objections to the ghost staying in the house as long as she did not harm our family. The ghost had kept its promise for seven years, until her alleged attack on my aunt.

My sister inquired what had happened to my aunt that night. My mother told her my aunt had woken up to someone sitting on her chest trying to choke her. My mother said it was the ghost. My aunt screamed, and when she did, the weight lifted, and she saw a figure running away from her bed. My mother felt betrayed by the ghost and decided to move her family from that house. That is why my mother insisted that my father build a new house for us, so that it would have no sordid past.

The conversation between my mother and sister defied all logic. However, it left an indelible impression on my psyche. The information I gathered on that day remained dormant for eight years, until one day it resurfaced and spooked me.

When I was seventeen, I was accepted at a prestigious medical school located ninety miles from our hometown. Two of my high school buddies had also been accepted there, so the three of us went to tour the new school and choose a dormitory. We could choose a room in either a newly constructed modern men's dorm with small rooms or an older men's dorm with bigger rooms. I picked the older dormitory, because it was located close to the girls' dormitory. My dormitory was the oldest building on campus, built in the Gothic style over a hundred years before. One of my buddies and I picked the largest room in the dormitory. Before classes started, we both spent time and money decorating our room.

The first semester we focused on anatomy, physiology, and biochemistry. The anatomy theater, where we dissected human bodies from head to toe, was a huge place with high ceilings and small windows. There were ten metal tables on either side of the room, and each one held a cadaver. The entire place smelled of formalin, the agent that preserved the bodies. The theater was located in a remote area of the campus, surrounded by tall trees and bushes. The place was well lit during the day but was stuffy because of the poor ventilation system. The location and the gloomy environment of the anatomy theater gave me the creeps. Even in the daytime, I never entered the theater on my own, and I never stayed there alone. I certainly never went there at night, even if someone was with me.

I enjoyed school very much. My parents were no longer looking over my shoulder, and all the guys in my dormitory got along well. The schoolwork was challenging, which I found satisfying because I was following my dream of becoming a doctor. Six months into the semester, after a grueling day, I returned to my room to find a note on my desk. My roommate and I belonged to different batches, so we did not see each other during the day. He had written that he would be away for several days to attend to a family emergency. He apologized for not being able to tell me in person. He would fill me in once he returned. Naturally, I was concerned about him and his family. We both hailed from the same hometown, and I knew his family well. I had no way of contacting him, however, since in those days few homes had telephones. I decided to grab dinner with my friends and relax for a bit. Around ten I came back to my room and did homework for an hour. Then I went to bed.

For the first time I was alone in the room at night. That fact didn't hit me until I turned off the light and rested my head on the pillow. I closed my eyes but could not sleep. Every now and then I would open my eyes and inspect the room without knowing what I was looking for. I tossed and turned, feeling every lump in the bed. In the past, I had gone to sleep without any difficulty. Now I was blaming my mattress. I barely slept the whole night, peeking every so often to see what time it was and hoping that I would fall asleep soon. The last time I checked the clock, it read 4:00 a.m. The next time, 7:00 a.m. Apparently I had managed to get a few hours of sleep.

I jumped out of bed, got dressed, and skipped breakfast in order to be in class by 7:30 sharp. Our physiology professor, an excellent teacher, was strict and accepted no excuse for tardiness. I liked his style of teaching and was always on time and attentive. However, on that day, as soon as I sat down, I dozed off within minutes. One of my classmates nudged me to wake me up. The whole day I could not focus on anything. I was exhausted and hungry.

I was eager to head back to my room and get a good night's rest. At the same time, the thought of spending another night alone in my room gave me the jitters. It was the first time I had ever felt butterflies flying wildly in my stomach. It was not even four in the afternoon, and I was already fretting over the night to come. I hung out with my friends, trying to have a good time and hoping that I would be able to face the night alone. Around eight, I returned to my room, saw my roommate's empty bed, and wished that he were back to rescue me from another disastrous night. I tried to read my textbooks, but I was only looking at the pages, and the information did not sink into my brain. The next three nights, I had trouble falling asleep. I would catch a half hour of sleep after tossing and turning for three to four hours and then wake up petrified that I had let my guard down. Every morning I was more exhausted. In the classroom, I began to select a corner seat in the back row so that my professor wouldn't notice if I snoozed.

On the fifth day of my roommate's absence, I went back to my room to find a letter from him. It said that his father had had a heart attack and was in critical condition. My roommate had decided to stay at home for another two weeks. He requested that I take his letter to the dean. While I was reading the letter, a strange chill came over me. I felt terrible about my friend's father, but I also felt terrible for my own selfish reasons. I knew that for the next two weeks, I would face rough nights. I realized at that moment that it was not just the next two weeks I had to worry about; the problem ran much deeper. The truth of the matter was that I was scared to sleep alone. I couldn't live my life like that. I had to figure out the exact nature of my sleeping problem and correct it immediately, otherwise not only would I flunk out of medical school, but I would also be incapacitated for the rest of my life.

While I pondered my problem, I dozed off. Around 12:30 a.m., I suddenly woke up frightened. My palms were sweating, I was hyperventilating, and my heart was pounding. My mind was saying, *How dare you go to sleep and leave me unguarded?* I knew I had to be vigilant throughout the night to protect myself, but from whom or what, I didn't know. The doors were made of solid wood, bolted from inside, and nearly impenetrable. And no one could climb through my windows because of the steel guards. But these facts failed to comfort me. The next night I was even more frightened to sleep alone in my room. I sat frozen in my bed for hours.

After seven sleepless nights, I spoke to a senior student in my dorm about my problems falling asleep. He consoled me and said that as a freshman it was natural to have disturbed sleep patterns. He explained that I was stressed out because the curriculum for incoming freshmen was demanding. He suggested that I take a mild sleeping pill, and he gave me a few from his stash. I was comforted knowing that I was not the only one who had problems sleeping. I also felt a lot calmer now that I had a solution to my problem.

I spent the next three hours preparing myself for a physiology test the next day. For the first time in a week, I was able to concentrate on my work. I took the pill at eleven and fell asleep within thirty minutes. When I woke up, it was 6:00 a.m. I jumped out of bed with joy, thrilled that I'd had a good night's rest. On the way to breakfast, I thanked my friend for his help.

The next two nights, the sleeping pills helped me to sleep well. On the third night, I woke up in the middle of the night shouting, "Get off my chest! Get off my chest!" I was sweating profusely and holding my throat with both hands to prevent it from being crushed. I sat up, looked around, and found no one in the room. I could not understand what had happened. Was it real, or was it a nightmare? I turned on the light, checked the room, and found no evidence of intrusion. Then it came back to me: my aunt's horrific experience in our old house nine years before and the conversation I had overheard between my mother and sister two years later. I really wished those events had never happened.

But I couldn't travel back in time to prevent them. I realized then that, deep down, I was afraid of ghosts. If I were ever to be free again to get a good night's sleep, I had to find a way to face my fear.

Unfortunately, my problem was as illogical and abstract as they come. If I suffered a physical ailment like pneumonia, it would be easy to understand and treat. I blamed myself for selecting a large room in an old building instead of a smaller room in a modern building. Probably if I had chosen the right dorm, I wouldn't be in this predicament. But deep down, I knew my problems had little to do with the room. The incident involving my aunt and the explanation offered by my mother had made their mark on my emotions.

Lack of sleep had worn me down. At this rate, I would be a nervous wreck by the end of the month. I knew I had to face my fears and resolve them—fast. But how? Before I could figure out the answers to my riddle, it was crucial that I understand it from the inside out. I decided to define my problem in a logical and scientific manner. My biggest problem was that I now seemed petrified of the dark because I felt that was when ghosts come out from hiding and hurt people. Did that mean I believed in ghosts? I must have, otherwise I would not be frightened of them. But what was I saying? A seventeen-year-old medical student who believed in ghosts! Logically it didn't make any sense—part of me doubted the existence of ghosts. But some younger, less rational part of me was convinced not only that they existed but also that they would strike against me as soon as I was alone and vulnerable. My mother had seen the ghost wandering in our old house, and she believed it had attacked my aunt. My love for my mother and my trust in her judgment won over logic, which led to my sleepless nights. I couldn't even close my eyes for fear that a ghost would choke me in my sleep.

At first, I could not come up with any way to tackle my fears. It took me days to come up with a few choices, all of which I rejected. I knew there was no magic pill for my problem. I had already decided not to take any more sleeping pills after my recent nightmare. I could try to locate a psychologist or psychiatrist with expertise in the field of ghosts. But even if I could locate such an expert, I was hesitant to make an appointment, because going to a psychiatrist in those days was taboo. I thought about seeking a spiritual guru who casts protection spells to ward off ghosts, but I ruled out that option because I didn't believe in such things. I considered asking my fellow medical students for guidance. Maybe they would come up with a sensible solution to my problem. Initially, I thought it was a brilliant idea, and then I thought about the ramifications of such a disclosure. Instead of getting help, I would most likely be ridiculed and might even have to leave school to save face.

My roommate had been gone for ten days, and I had still not come up with a sensible solution to my problem. Just when I was about to throw in the towel, it occurred to me that a sensible, conventional plan would not work to solve such a bizarre problem. Maybe a radical and unconventional weapon would help me to conquer my fears. I remembered the phrase "Fight fire with fire," and the spirit of the idea appealed to me. I decided to take on the ghost on its turf rather than waiting for it to attack me in my room.

While I was contemplating my strategy, I remembered a story I'd heard a month before from a waiter at a nearby café. In fact, now that I thought of it, the story might have precipitated the frantic feelings that had surfaced when I found myself alone at night in my room. Just a block away from the campus, there was a cozy garden café perched on a slight rise overlooking the center of the city. Many medical students went there, as the food was decent and affordable. I had gone to the café one afternoon to have a cool drink. When the familiar middle-aged waiter took my order, I noticed that he was sweating and appeared tired, which made sense, as the day was hot and humid. The café was practically empty that day, and out of pity I offered to buy him a cool drink. Besides, I wanted company.

He thanked me for the drink and sat down across from me. Our conversation took many twists and turns. I learned that he was forty-eight years old and single and that he lived alone. He held two jobs: during the day he waited tables at the café, and at night, he was one of two night watchmen at the medical school. I was curious to know how he passed the time, watching over such a desolate place. He surprised me by saying that he enjoyed his night job because he didn't have a supervisor looking over his shoulder. He also said that he met some interesting characters at night. Curious as to what he might mean, I encouraged him to say more. He said that his main job as a night watchman was to turn off all the lights and secure the administrative offices. He checked to make sure the doors to all the other buildings were closed. And he would make rounds of the campus several times during the night. The rest of the time he stayed in his office.

I prodded him about the interesting characters he met at night. He smirked and said, "They are not the regular kind of people you might think of."

"What do you mean?" I asked.

"Even if I tell you," he said, "you won't believe me. Just like your friends from the school. They make fun of me. But I know what I know."

"I promise I won't make fun of you," I said.

He thought about my assurance for a few seconds and then began to speak. Ten years ago, he said, the first night on the job, he went to the night watchman's office at the medical school, took a flashlight, and patrolled the campus. There were a few lights on in the chemistry lab, which he turned off. After rounding the campus, he went back to the office, sat down, and started to sip from a cup of coffee and read a tabloid newspaper. Around midnight, he began his second round, and as he neared the anatomy theater he heard the sound of sobbing.

He wondered who would want to come to the anatomy theater at that time of the night. Of course he would check it out and see what the person was doing. When he got closer to the theater, he could tell that the sounds were coming from inside the building. There were no lights on inside, since the watchman had turned off the main switch earlier. He opened the door and shone his flashlight around the theater. To his surprise, he didn't see anyone inside, and though the crying had stopped, he could hear the sound of two voices whispering in the far corner. He shone his flashlight toward the corner and saw no one, other than the mutilated dead bodies lying on the tables. He was puzzled. Maybe some students were pulling a prank on him. A few seconds later, he saw two shadows moving from one table to another. Ghosts!

He ran back to his office, locked his door, and tried to make sense of his close encounter with another realm. He needed the job badly, because it was his only job at the time. In the morning, as soon as his shift was over, he dashed to the nearest temple and spoke to a priest whom he knew well. The cleric was sympathetic to his plight and gave him a sacred seed from a banyan tree on a saffron-colored thread. "Carry this," he said, "and it will protect you."

Since then he'd always worn it. He still heard noises coming from the anatomy theater, loudest at the new moon, when the night was darkest. Because of the power of that sacred seed, however, the ghosts never bothered him. His story had definitely struck a chord in me, and when he looked at my face to see my reaction, instead of laughing at him, I nodded and said he might be right, without explaining my own encounter with the supernatural when I was seven years old.

A month later, in the wake of all my sleepless nights, I considered that the night watchman's ghost story and the absence of my room-mate might have triggered my own latent fear of ghosts. Once I made these connections, my battle plan became clear to me. I would nip my fears in the bud and refuse to let them incapacitate me ever again. At midnight of the next new moon, three days away, I would invade the anatomy theater, and it would serve as my battleground. But what kinds of weapons would have the maximum lethal impact on ghosts? After some thought, I decided to take a knife, a wooden staff five feet long and two inches in diameter, and a flashlight. (Even now I chuckle at my choice of weapons. What can I say? I was seventeen; I didn't know any better.) I thought about recruiting the night watchman to guide me in my endeavor but rejected the idea because it was my fight, not his. What if the battle became ugly or dangerous? Besides, if he didn't keep my plans a secret, all the other students would tease me forever. No, I decided to tackle my enemy alone.

Once I had decided on a strategy, I was a lot calmer than I had been before. I even managed to catch a little sleep. On the Friday of the new moon I woke up at 6:00 a.m., showered, and went to the temple to say a prayer. I attended classes and followed my daily routine, return-ing to my room at six that evening. I had no appetite, so I didn't eat anything. Six more hours until midnight. I decided to stay in the room alone. As the hour approached, I dressed in jeans and a T-shirt, picked up my switchblade, and tucked it into my belt. Once again I checked the batteries in the flashlight. At 11:45 I left my room. I looked around to make sure that there was no one around. Sometimes when the days were hot and humid, my friends and I would pull chairs out of our rooms and spend hours in the breezy corridor, but on that particular night, the corridor was deserted. There was a slight chill in the air, which was unusual for that time of year. I set out for the anatomy theater, a twelve-minute walk from my dorm.

I was scared stiff. Once I entered the battleground, there would be no turning back. I had no idea about the number and strength of the ghosts. I might be hurt or even killed. But at seventeen I already knew that life is fraught with uncertainties; there are no guarantees. If I wished to live free from the fear of ghosts for the rest of my life, I had to be willing to risk my life. I would carry out my plan and let Nature take its course.

The theater doors were never locked. I pushed the door open and stood outside, listening. I heard nothing inside the theater. Three minutes later, I pushed the door open further and took a peek inside. I swept the huge room with my flashlight beam but saw no movement. Finally, I mustered all my courage and stepped into the battleground. I tried to calm my racing heart by placing my right hand on my chest. I was holding the wooden staff in my right hand and the flashlight in my left. I was sweating from head to toe. I stood for some time near the door. After a short while, my eyes began to adjust to the darkness inside the theater. I swept the flashlight across the room again. There were no signs of ghosts, just the cadavers lying motionless on their tables and the closed-in stench of formalin in the air. I moved toward the middle of the theater, expecting the ghosts to attack me at any moment, but nothing happened. For the next fifteen minutes, I stood scanning the theater for any sound or movement. Not even a mouse was stirring. I thought maybe the ghosts were taunting me. Once I let my guard down, they would certainly attack me, or even worse, they would possess the disfigured bodies and charge toward me. I had seen a scary movie recently called *Zombies*, in which corpses attacked people in the middle of the night. But another fifteen minutes passed, and the theater remained quiet.

I became less and less vigilant as time passed. Forty minutes later, I actually began to get bored. I shouted into the empty room and dared the ghosts to show up, thinking that the tone in my voice would flush them out. But my words did not have any effect on the quiet room. I began to think that ghosts didn't exist. What if they were just figments of the imagination? But then I thought of my mother, who did believe in ghosts. I didn't want to disrespect her beliefs, but under the circumstances, I had to tell myself that both she and my aunt were superstitious individuals with active imaginations. I could not explain their experiences or my own in any other way. If a ghost wanted to hurt my aunt, couldn't it have done so without letting her make such a racket? The more I thought about the incidence that had taken place so many years before, the more I was convinced that my aunt had had a nightmare rather than a ghostly encounter, perhaps spurred by my mother's tales of a ghostly inhabitant in our house.

I began to feel good about myself for having the courage to take action against my fears instead of succumbing to them. Around 1:15 a.m. I decided to head back to my room like a conqueror. When I stepped out of the anatomy theater, I stopped looking over my shoulder for ghosts forever. When I entered my room, I was exhausted and sweaty. I took a refreshing shower, gulped down a glass of cold water, and went to bed. When I opened my eyes again, my alarm clock read 2:00 p.m. I panicked for a moment—my first instinct was to get up and race to class. Then I realized it was Saturday. If not for the flashlight, the wooden staff, and the knife lying on the table in my room, I would have thought the previous night's experience had been a dream. I sat up in bed and leaned back on the headboard. I was still in a daze, but I was exuberant. When I thought about what I had done, I could not contain my happiness.

There was a knock on the door, and when I answered it I found two smiling friends who wanted to know if I would join them for a snack at the café. They were surprised to see me still dressed in my pajamas. I lied and said that I had pulled an all-nighter studying for an upcoming test. I dressed, and we went to the café, choosing a corner table near a big window. Our familiar waiter greeted us and took our order. When he left our table, my two friends snickered. I looked at them questioningly.

"We have a nickname for him," one friend said. "It's Goofy Ghost Man."

"You know that he's a night watchman at the school?" the other friend asked, and I nodded. "Well, after he ends his shift here and before he starts his night shift at the school, he makes a little trip to the liquor store."

"We've wondered how he can perform his duties in that condition," the first friend said.

"Has he told you the story about the sobbing ghosts in the anatomy theater?" the other friend asked.

Again, I nodded.

"We think it's the alcohol playing tricks."

No wonder I hadn't seen any ghosts. I felt sorry for the waiter and thanked my lucky stars I had decided not to include him in my plans.

That night I didn't have the slightest trepidation about spending the night alone in my room.

My experience fighting ghosts illustrated that I was terrified of the unknown. In fact, fear of the unknown is a primal fear many of us experience in different forms. Fear of the unknown strikes a spark that results in a wildfire of insecurity, one of the main stimuli that causes stress. When we allow our imaginations to run wild in areas where the truth is unknown or unknowable, our fantasies can override good sense and take control of our lives. I learned to take any information I heard with a grain of salt, think it over, and even double-check it before accepting it as fact. Based on my experience—and in spite of what I learned from my beloved mother and what I heard from the waiter at the café—I am 99 percent sure that ghosts do not exist, and if they do, I am 100 percent sure they are more afraid of me than I am of them.

Ultimately, this experience helped me understand that the best way to meet any threat is head-on, with courage, clarity, and confidence. It reminded me that all problems have solutions. To properly assess how serious a threat is, we need facts, but identifying the facts among all the information we receive is easier said than done. Our minds are known to play tricks on us, and sometimes the answers to our most compelling questions (Has God abandoned me? Do ghosts really exist?) are not available to us. That some things will always be unknowable is something we must accept. Some threats feel like life and death, causing fear and panic—the emotions I had to face before I could assess the threat of ghosts, a threat that at the time felt very real to me. Through my own experiences and those of my patients, I have come to understand that the root cause of the tension we think of as stress is our unwillingness to face our deepest fears. Having courage means facing and fighting against those things that scare us most. Desperate situations call for bold solutions.

Threats come in all forms and from all directions. They touch all aspects of our lives. As you set the stage and begin to devise a strategy to conquer the stress in your life, consider the areas where you feel the most threatened. Consider the origins of these threats. The following questions can help you face any threat with courage, clarity, and confidence:

1. What is the threat you face? Is it internal or external, implied or imminent, real or perceived, logical or illogical?
2. What about this threat feels real to you right now?
3. What facts do you know about the threat?
4. Is the threat illogical in any way? If yes, explain how. Is it possible the threat might be imaginary?
5. Can you tell what kind of fear is at the root of the threat? Fear of death, abandonment, the unknown, poverty?
6. What are some ways you can face this threat, whether it is logical or illogical, real or perceived?

Let us look at a few examples to illustrate the effective analysis of the threats in our lives:

EXAMPLE 1: You are a soldier in the US armed forces deployed to a war zone in Afghanistan. You have sworn to uphold the honor, allegiance, and security of your country. You know that on the front line you will either kill or be killed; there is no middle ground. But taking the lives of others has an emotional price. It is only natural to feel guilty, sad, or scared when facing these circumstances. The threat to your life is external, real, and imminent, so your fear of death is not irrational but quite appropriate.

How can your protect your sanity and safety under such circumstances?

1.  Focus on what's happening in the moment and on responding appropriately. When in a combat zone, for example, it is appropriate to be on guard as much as physically possible. When on leave or administrative duty, such vigilance does not serve a realistic or logical purpose.
2.  Allow your instincts to tell you which of your fellow soldiers you can trust.
3.  Kill only if necessary to save your own life or the life of a comrade.
4.  Whenever possible, disable and capture your enemy, and let your superiors deal with the captives.
5.  Be proud for serving your country to the best of your ability.
6.  Keep in touch with family members. Back home, your family feels the threat of your imminent death as well. They are helpless and restless, wondering if you'll ever return home, and if you do, if you'll be in good physical health and of sound mind. It is up to you to assure them that you are being vigilant. In return, they can give you the love and support you need.

EXAMPLE 2: You have a premonition of dying while driving your car or traveling in a plane. Now you're scared to get into a car or a plane. You feel the threat to your life in this situation is external, imminent, real, and logical, but it is actually internal, implied, perceived, and illogical. The threat feels external, but actually your imagination and your insecurities have teamed up to create an internal threat. Your imagination has persuaded you that the threat of death is imminent when the threat is actually only implied, as it is any time you drive your car or travel by plane.

Let us say, on the other hand, that the external implied threat becomes imminent and you have a close encounter with death while traveling by car or plane. And let's say that the experience leaves you convinced that if you ride in a car or an airplane again, you will surely die. Feeling this way after that kind of experience is a sure sign you are suffering from post-traumatic stress disorder (PTSD). You might feel that the best way to deal with the threat is to run away from it; however, the truth is that the more you run, the harder the threat will bear down on you.

In either situation, if you want to enjoy a stress-free life, you must face the facts with courage, recognize the true nature of the threat with clarity, and take appropriate action with confidence. First, face the fact that no one can avoid death. Second, understand that you have only so much control over the threats related to contemporary modes of travel. You can't control the mechanical condition of an airplane, for example, but you can choose an airline with a strong safety record. You can't control the other drivers on the road, but you can be a defensive driver. Once you've taken appropriate measures to protect your safety, stop fretting over the threats over which you have no control, and focus on living a meaningful life.

EXAMPLE 3: You suspect that your spouse is cheating on you, which makes you feel insecure and rejected, which in turn leads you to question whether you should stay in your marriage. Should you confront your spouse? Try to find evidence to support your suspicions? Give up and file for divorce? The threat could be external or internal, implied or imminent, real or perceived, logical or illogical. Most important, you do not trust your spouse, and without trust, a marriage isn't worth much.

Marriage is like a plant that needs constant nurturing from both partners to keep its foliage healthy and colorful. It is irrelevant what your spouse may or may not have done behind your back if you were doing less than your part of the nurturing in the marriage. Before you confront your spouse, you must face the facts of your current situation with courage. Do you want your marriage to succeed? Are you willing to invest the care and attention needed to save your marriage? If, after examining your own feelings honestly, you decide that saving your marriage is not a priority for you and you recognize and accept the price you will pay by dissolving it, then dissolve it.

On the contrary, if you are committed to doing your part to save your marriage, invite your spouse to have an honest and open dialogue with you. Allow your spouse to express his or her true feelings and concerns about the marriage, and in turn, express your own. At this point, neither of you has anything to lose, with your marriage at such a low point. If you find you and your spouse are equally committed to saving your relationship, set aside your own suspicions and clear the way to build a stronger bond between the two of you. If you are serious about strengthening your marriage, both partners must put aside petty differences and focus on the strengths that each of you brings to the relationship. This is the first step toward making your marriage the spiritual partnership it was meant to be. In my opinion, marriage is conceived by the union of two bodies and sustained by the union of two souls.

EXAMPLE 4: You are always careful with your finances, never spending beyond your means, and now you have enough set aside to make some investments. You hesitate, however, because you are nervous about trusting someone else with your hard-earned money. You've heard many stories about people who have lost their life savings and their retirement money through failed investments and unscrupulous investment agents. You've also heard about banks failing. The more you think about it, the more you wonder if you should just keep your money in cash, hidden under your mattress.

You interpret the threat in this case as external, imminent, and real, while it is actually external, implied, and real. It is true that you gamble whenever you invest money in the stock market, so due caution is warranted. But it's illogical to assume that because some people have lost the money they've invested, you will too. Millions of people invest their money wisely and use their gains to retire comfortably. You can do it too, if you trust your instincts more than your emotions when considering how and where to invest your money. Always follow these sound, time-tested investment principles:

1.  If an investment opportunity seems too good to be true, it most likely *is* too good to be true. Proceed with caution or seek out other options.
2.  Never put all your eggs in one basket.
3.  Pay attention to what's happening in the world of finance. You don't have to be an expert to learn from stock market upheavals and financial debacles, and the information will help you to become a savvy investor.
4.  Find a financial adviser you can trust and who understands your

financial priorities and goals. Get recommendations from friends or other financial professionals you know. Ask for references and talk to some of the adviser's current long-term customers.

5. Even after you find a financial adviser you can trust, take his or her recommendations with a grain of salt. Gather as much information as possible independently, consider your options, and then take action that seems appropriate to you. After all, only you are truly responsible for your own money.

6. If you decide that you just can't accept the threats inherent in stock-market investments, deposit your funds in savings bonds or a savings account guaranteed by the Federal Deposit Insurance Corporation (FDIC). The interest yield may be low, but your money is safe and will grow slowly over the years.

EXAMPLE 5: You are a small business owner in a difficult economy. Your profit is declining while your expenses are rising. Between overhead expenses, irate customers, and employee conflicts, you're beginning to feel as though your business can't possibly survive. The threats you face are external, imminent, and real, and your reaction is logical: you are stressed out because your patience and peace of mind are constantly being tested. The fear of failure has brought you unprecedented levels of stress.

What is the solution to conquering your stress? First, take solace in the fact that in an ever-changing world, most small business owners have experienced the same frustration, sorrow, and helplessness you're feeling. Then, with courage, face the fact that you have only two options when faced with stress: you can change the situation to your liking, or you can accept and adjust to the situation. You cannot change the economy, so you're going to have to accept and adjust to the situation. Accepting the situation means choosing either fight or flight. Either you rally and figure out some innovative ways to save your business, or you close your doors and, if necessary, declare bankruptcy.

Building a successful business is hard, but maintaining it is even harder. Before you decide to throw in the towel, analyze your business practices to make sure you're operating as efficiently and successfully as possible, using the following questions as a guide:

1. Are you built to roll with the punches? Changes are the norm in the business world.
2. Are you patient, proactive, and persistent? Are you constantly looking for ways to innovate your business practices?
3. Even when business improves, do you keep your expenses low and put money aside for unexpected emergencies?
4. Are you self-reliant? Are you extremely cautious about expanding your business or taking on new partners?
5. Are you kind to your employees without allowing them to abuse your kindness? A loyal, hardworking employee is an invaluable asset.
6. Do you fire unreliable employees? They are costing you money.
7. Do you keep your promises? A good reputation and credibility are the crux of any successful business. Always try to deliver goods or services to your customers on time.

If you follow these principles, you never need lose sleep over your business, because you will know you are running it to the best of your abilities. I am the owner of a small business and have weathered many storms. After I became the chairman of the anesthesia department at a local hospital, I began to build a behavior modification clinic, seeing patients in the evenings and on Saturdays. I am patient and passionate about my work. I am always looking for newer and better ways to treat my patients, because I care for them and want to do the best for them. At the same time, I am also always looking for better ways to enhance my financial security, knowing that my business must be financially successful to survive. Therefore, I have to be both a competent physician and a savvy businessman.

Each day, everyone is bombarded by threats to our safety and well-being—death, insecurity, failure, rejection—which cause the tension we call stress. The good news is that when we learn to evaluate these threats with courage, clarity, and confidence, we invalidate the vast majority of them. We can only control so much in this difficult world, and we can only protect ourselves in limited ways from those things that are out of our control. What is out of our control, we must accept and adjust to. We must then face each viable threat head-on in order to trace the source of the stress to its root and vanquish it for good. Courage is the nemesis of any threat.

*Three*

---

# Tuning In to the Laws of Nature

Ever since humans became self-aware, we have wondered about our creator. Who designed the universe? How do we explain our existence? What is the nature of the energy that animates our bodies (our souls)? What factors determine the time, place, and circumstances of our arrival and departure from this earth? In spite of advancements in science and technology, we have yet to fathom the basic secrets of Nature. Consider a simple concept like gravity, which took a long time for us to theorize. Even now, we are unable to explain the source of gravity and the dark matter that prevails in the universe.

When we recognize the sheer number of inexplicable aspects surrounding us, in our own world and beyond, most of us conclude that there is a force much greater than us at work. Belief and faith in a higher power is part of human cultures the world over, despite the absence of absolute proof of its existence. We all need a spiritual reference point to guide our thoughts and actions—even an atheist most likely has faith in the power of the Higher Self. Faith in a higher power provides an anchor for our thoughts and encourages us to care for ourselves and to think of how our actions affect other living beings. I call this higher power "Nature" or "Our Maker," and I believe it is responsible for creating, regulating, and managing the universe and its inhabitants. When you are ready to set the stage for your battle against stress, your first task is to acknowledge Nature (Our Maker) and its tenets. Once we acknowledge Nature and understand its attributes, we can see the options Nature offers to rid our lives of stress.

Let us now, regardless of our individual religious beliefs, entertain the possibility that the force that made us is an enigmatic, eternal, invisible but invincible entity with an agenda of its own: justice in its purest form, light in its brightest form, energy in its cleanest form, and truth in its absolute form. Our Maker is the one and only perfect force that permeates the universe. Its domain is beyond our comprehension. Our Maker, Nature, is not human or humanoid. It has neither a physical form nor a compassionate disposition. We are accountable to Nature, not the other way around. As we saw with my patient Gina, we are bound for disappointment and acute stress when we expect Nature (God) to be accountable to us.

Nature has set terms and conditions for the existence of this world and its inhabitants. Its priorities are not the same as ours. For instance, species have come and gone over the ages, but life has continued to exist in one form or another. While we should care about the preservation of other species to protect our own interests and the balance of life on our planet, we should also understand that Nature is concerned not with any specific life form, but only with the existence of life.

It is in our best interest to understand Nature as it exists and relate to it on its terms. If we begin with the premise that Nature is a perfect force, then we understand that forgiveness is not a necessary part of its vocabulary. Forgiveness is in fact a human rather than a divine characteristic. Because we are human and thus imperfect, it is guaranteed that we will make mistakes. Resolution of our inevitable mistakes does not come from Nature; the only resolution of which we imperfect beings are capable is to acknowledge what we have done wrong, correct it if possible, and learn a valuable lesson from it. Most important, we must endure the consequences of our mistakes with courage and strength. Finally, when we make mistakes, we must forgive ourselves and one another and move forward. We must strive to be perfect like Nature but at the same time understand that we never will reach that goal. As we saw with two of my patients, the hypochondriac Harold and the golf enthusiast John, when we expect to be perfect, we create acute stress in our lives. It must be enough for us to improve—to learn and grow—knowing that perfection is not possible in this lifetime.

It is not uncommon or unrealistic, however, to expect our hard work to pay off while we're alive, although we must keep in mind that Nature's awareness of time is vastly different from our own. The time between a human birth and a human death is a speck compared to eternity. Indeed, future generations often reap the benefits of a current generation's hard work. We must understand that despite all our efforts, progress may be delivered to us piecemeal or otherwise not in the manner we expect or desire. Building beautiful lives for ourselves while also trying to make this world a better place may take a very long time, because progress is scheduled on Nature's timeline, not on ours. Once we realize the nature of progress, we are suddenly able to keep sight of the noblest of goals, to move forward with patience rather than disappointment or discouragement. Acknowledging Nature helps us to let go of those things we cannot control and focus instead on the process, on being happy in our daily lives rather than stressing over the final outcome.

We can tune into Nature's general qualities by observing how the world works. For example, life is persistent and variegated under the best circumstances and even persists under circumstances we might think would discourage it, such as poverty and a polluted environment. From this observation, we might draw the conclusion that Nature is concerned with life in a general sense. We can thus guarantee our own survival as a species if we follow Nature's mandates to create the optimum conditions for life to persist.

Based on my observations of how the world works, I have deduced several more of Nature's general recommendations:

*Respect your body.* If you expect your body to serve you well, take good care of it by eating healthily and exercising regularly (for at least thirty minutes every day). Understand that even when you take good care of yourself, you are still vulnerable to diseases and conditions caused by genetic and environmental factors, which are out of your control.

*Know your mind.* Keep your brain clear by avoiding chemical pollutants. Explore the instinctual, intellectual, and emotional aspects of your mind (see below) and understand which aspect should lead under particular circumstances.

*Learn to respect your fellow human beings.* They have the same rights as you to live in this world. The concerns of the individual are important, but we are also dependent on each other for survival.

*Know your strengths, weaknesses, and limitations, and review them before engaging with this world.* Face and resolve the internal threats that cause you stress and only then work to settle your differences with the outside world.

*Focus on developing good habits.* All it takes is one bad habit to shorten your life.

*Consider the possible results of your actions before you act.* Consider whether your actions will reflect your values and solve your problems. Consider whether your actions will be effective and efficient.

*Learn from your past and apply that knowledge to your present actions to secure a sound future.*

*Work individually and with others to keep our air, water, and land as free of pollutants as possible.* Pollution threatens our survival as a species.

*Train your children to be strong, sensible, intuitive, and self-reliant.* Train them to tune in to Nature.

## THE THREE ASPECTS OF THE MIND

In addition to deducing Nature's general laws through observation, we can also connect with Nature on a personal level, which allows us to gain valuable insight into Nature's terms and conditions for our daily existence. There is no guidebook for connecting with Nature this way; we must think and feel our way toward an interpretation of the laws of Nature that apply specifically to our own lives. Each of us is unique, and we each have a unique relationship with Nature. No one can see my strengths and weakness, my hopes and dreams as clearly as I can when I look at myself honestly and rationally. We create stress when we lie to ourselves about our abilities, our responsibilities, and what dreams we might actually realize in this lifetime. It is when we tune in to Nature that we become comfortable with ourselves and able to work with rather than against the gifts and limitations Nature has provided.

In the animal kingdom, a cheetah hunts for certain animals, such as gazelle, rather than other animals, such as lions or elephants, for its meal. It instinctively knows its limitations and the strengths of other animals in its habitat. It would be detrimental to the cheetah to overestimate its capacities and underestimate the strength of its competitors. The cheetah's speed, agility, determination, patience, and unbiased understanding of its limitations serve the animal well.

As human beings we too must construct an objective understanding of our limitations. For instance, if you aspire to be a professional basketball player but are only 5'2", the likelihood of fulfilling such a dream is unrealistic, because you're simply not tall enough. If you're in tune with Nature and the gifts it has given to you, you can appreciate the game of basketball while exploring opportunities in a different sport that is more suited to your strengths. The irony is that once you accept your limitations and weaknesses, that acceptance is added to the list of your strengths. When we voluntarily assess, acknowledge, and accept our strengths and limitations, we no longer feel failure and disappointment.

Like cheetahs, humans have sound instincts. But what sets us apart from other animals is the mind. Our minds enable us to be self-conscious, aware of our instinct, our intellect, and our emotions. Thus, for humans, the process of identifying our strengths and weaknesses is more complicated than it is for other animals. In order to live stress-free, we must first have a thorough working knowledge of the ways in which these three aspects of our minds—instinct, intellect, and emotion—work in a dynamic relationship with one another.

It may seem absurd that we have to make time to understand ourselves when we live with ourselves every day. However, it is an important investment in your future to define your strengths, your shortcomings, your talents, your priorities, and your expectations. Your personal views should be crystal clear to you, and you should have a strong sense of who you are and how you are different from others. In order to evaluate yourself accurately, you must first understand the dynamics of your mind—that mysterious entity capable of both stressing you out and devising ingenious maneuvers to help you to survive in a harsh and ever-changing world. I developed my Turning Point Program in hopes of helping people balance the three aspects of the mind, thereby easing stress. In practice, I have found that the program opens barriers and develops a channel of free communication between them.

THE INSTINCTUAL MIND: The instinctual aspect of the mind is located in the unconscious, the part of the mind of which we are most often unaware as we live our daily lives. This part of the mind, through which Nature's laws are expressed, plays a crucial role in our survival because it holds three basic directives from Nature:

1. Protect life
2. Preserve the surrounding environment to support life
3. Propagate life

These fundamental directives operate in our minds as basic instincts to secure shelter, to eat, to drink, and to procreate. However, Nature has also made this division of the mind home to countless acquired or learned habits that help us fulfill Nature's directives.

Instinctive behavior is much more prevalent in lower-order animals than it is in humans. Lower-order animals' learning capacity is limited by their meager intellect and narrow range of emotions. Humans' learned behavior, conversely, is capable both of overshadowing instinctual behavior and of modifying it. On an individual basis, we are even capable of interpreting Nature's directives and then choosing which habits we'd like to acquire in order to carry them out. For example, behaviors such as swimming, hunting, flying, and climbing come naturally to lower-order animals to ensure their survival. Beyond these instinctive behaviors, they acquire few learned habits. A chimpanzee might use a stick as a tool to lure ants for its meal, and a monkey might break a coconut on a rock in order to eat the flesh, but these habits serve specific purposes of survival. Humans have a wide range of learned behaviors that go beyond subsistence, including driving cars, flying airplanes, swimming, riding bicycles, typing, even Tweeting.

In the animal kingdom, Nature determines mating rituals, and the sole purpose of mating for the vast majority of animals is to reproduce and guarantee the survival of their species. However, human beings are not bound by such restrictions. We do have an instinctive drive to procreate, but this drive is mitigated by the fact that humans also seek out sexual intimacy for pleasure alone, a characteristic shared by a few other species of mammal.[1] Our desire for sex is also influenced by the intellectual and emotional divisions of our minds. Over time, human beings have developed cultural rituals and birth control so that we now have the freedom to choose when to have sex and when to start a family. This freedom of choice is paired with responsibility. When people indulge in the freedom without acknowledging the responsibility, everyone involved suffers. For example, when a couple desires physical intimacy for pleasure alone but takes no precautions against sexually transmitted infections or unwanted pregnancy, one of these unwanted results will often occur. On the other hand, when sexual partners decide they want a baby, they also have responsibilities, including making sure they've chosen the right partner and selecting the best time to bring the child into the world.

In this day and age, the expectations of civilization and culture often cause us to lose touch with our instincts; we are often able to mediate primal emotions such as fear, pleasure, and anger with our intellects. However, we still need to be in touch with our instincts if we are to tune in to Nature. Our instincts are a vital component of our minds when used in cooperation with the intellectual and emotional divisions. For example, our instincts are indispensable in helping us understand Nature's mandates and how best to follow them in our lives.

THE INTELLECTUAL MIND: The human intellect is the conscious part of the mind. It is responsible for absorbing and analyzing the barrage of sensory information we receive from the environment and recommending appropriate responses. Of the three divisions of the mind, it is most in touch with the outside world, and we see the world through it. It is the division of which we are most aware as we go about our daily duties. It is composed of rational functions including reasoning, judgment, logic, discretion, calculation, imagination, analysis, and anticipation. It is the most complex and evolved section of the mind. When you allow the instincts in cooperation with the intellect to lead in most matters, you will enjoy an unfettered freedom from stress for the rest of your life.

If we were all given the same intellectual gifts by Nature and the input from the environment were processed only in the intellectual division of our minds, without any interference or influence from the instinctual or emotional divisions, our impressions of the world would be uniform and universal. Even people of diverse ethnic and geographical backgrounds would interpret a similar environment in the same way. There would be no conflict and therefore no stress. But in reality, while many of us possess similar intellectual abilities, Nature has not given the same gifts to everyone. Both genetics and our life experiences make our minds different from one another. No two people have exactly the same interests or make exactly the same connections between data. We see the same set of facts from individual perspectives. Such diversity is also greatly influenced by the emotional division of the mind.

THE EMOTIONAL MIND: The emotional division of the mind consists of two subdivisions—primitive emotions and advanced emotions. Primitive emotions originate in the unconscious and include rage, pain, pleasure, comfort, thrill, fear, grief, and selfishness. Humans share the capacity for primitive emotions with almost all larger (macroscopic) terrestrial organisms. Advanced emotions—which originate in the conscious realm—include love, caring, affection, passion, compassion, concern, deceit, jealousy, hatred, greed, pride, and prejudice. We share advanced emotions with higher-order animal species, such as primates and cetaceans. Higher intelligence in a species corresponds with a wider range of advanced emotions. Human beings display the widest range of advanced emotions of any species on Earth.

The influence of different emotions on the mind varies between individuals, resulting in the unique personal view each of us holds. In some people, fear and rage have a stronger influence than compassion and tolerance. In others, love and caring mute the influence of greed and jealousy. The emotional mind has a strong influence on an individual's overall disposition, attitude, outlook, and behavior. In fact, it is the emotional mind that shapes each person's response to the environment and creates the motivation to act. Emotions are the policy makers of the human mind. To illustrate this point, let us consider a couple of examples. Several educated, experienced, and knowledgeable Wall Street executives and hedge fund managers acted with impunity despite knowing the consequences associated with Ponzi schemes, sub-prime mortgages, and highly inflated structured investment vehicles. If their intellect alone had been the policy maker for their actions, they would not have engaged in such risky investment strategies, for the intellect would have understood easily that the risks outweighed any possible benefit. We would have avoided the 2008 stock market crash, the collapse of many financial institutions, and the subsequent massive unemployment. Many executives would have preserved their wealth, their comfortable family lives, their peace of mind, and their freedom. However, greed, arrogance, selfishness, and the thrill of immediate gratification overruled their intellect. These emotions were the policy makers in their minds and drove them to act foolishly and egregiously. My mother once said that people who chase fame and fortune eventually live in regret, and this explains why.

Consider also the example of a powerful politician who cheats on his spouse and jeopardizes his reputation, credibility, future prospects, and family life all for an illicit thrill. His actions are motivated by his emotional mind, which demands instant gratification without respect for the cost. If the politician's intellect were the policy maker, he would not risk all the things he has taken a lifetime to build.

However, not all emotions are detrimental to the individual or the people around him. There are countless incidences where people have come to the rescue of others, saving them from the jaws of death or providing food, shelter, and comfort. Emotions such as compassion, care, and love are the motivators for such noble actions. In fact, without emotions, human beings would be mostly passive, only acting in response to instinctive urges or environmental stimulus. With emotions working in conjunction with the instinctual mind and the intellectual mind, we have the option of acting or remaining passive, depending on how we evaluate the situation.

Emotions by themselves are intrinsically associative and irrational. While they are sometimes connected to instinct, as in the fight or flight response, they do not follow the same rules as either the instinctual or the intellectual divisions of the mind. For example, my patient John's emotional reaction to flying was out of proportion to the actual risks involved with airplane travel. For him, flying triggered the primitive fear of death. Primitive emotions such as fear, rage, and despair feel much more powerful than advanced emotions or intellectual thoughts. The human propensity to wage war is motivated by the survival instinct combined with the emotional misinterpretation that insists that territory is worth killing and dying for and that there are no alternatives to violence to reach certain goals. These rationalizations for war come with no help from the intellect.

An imbalance between the emotions, the intellect, and the instincts leads to stress. When we respond to stress by making a decision based on emotion alone, we can be sure of more stress, in the form of negative consequences. For example, a smoker's intellectual mind tells her that cigarettes are bad for her health and that the pleasure of smoking is not worth the cost in health problems. But she will not succeed at quitting smoking until she accepts these facts on an emotional level—until she believes. While the intellect is the realm of facts, the emotional division of the mind is the realm of belief. Our beliefs rather than our knowledge drive us to take action. In this case, the lopsided emotional division is allowed free reign to pursue pleasure and the thrill of danger, and the person decides to continue smoking. The conflicting agenda between the intellect and emotion causes stress.

While every emotion we possess has a crucial role to play, balance is key. For instance, jealousy has the reputation of a leper. But a touch of jealousy inspires us to best the competition. On the other hand, jealousy that overpowers the intellect and the instincts causes us to lose sight of right and wrong and spurs us to action that is likely to produce disastrous results. Similarly, fear is an appropriate reaction in a dangerous environment and encourages us to use caution or to defend ourselves. But fear allowed to rule the other divisions of the mind can incapacitate us, leaving us physically and intellectually paralyzed when we need to act.

When certain emotions—including guilt, desperation, and vengeance—prompt action, the result is never positive. Guilt is the sadness we feel when we perceive that we have made a mistake. It is important to recognize the origin and source of our guilt—which are like two peas in a pod—in order to move beyond it. Guilt originates in our perception that we have crossed the line between right and wrong. The source of guilt is more specific. For instance, those of us who are overly sensitive, sentimental, compassionate, and generous may feel guilty for not doing enough to stop the pain and suffering of others—whether in relation to homelessness, world hunger, or other social ills. In such cases, an overzealous, good-hearted nature has prompted an irrational response. Our guilt blinds us to one of our limitations as human beings—specifically that we cannot help everyone to our satisfaction. Instead, we must balance our irrational goals and unrealistic desires with the kinds of sensible and rational ideas that allow us to do what we can and feel satisfied by our actions.

Indulging guilt is pointless, because it is a bottomless pit. Not one of us can undo a mistake we have made or ever do enough to help the needy of this world, so to dwell on these things is a pointless waste of time and energy. Guilt triggers stress in the form of self-loathing and self-deprecation. It encourages self-pity. Persistent guilt produces an overpowering sense of inferiority, which can lead to alcohol and drug addiction.

How do we disconnect from guilt and move forward? Having made a specific mistake, we have several choices. We may, at the first sign of remorse, attempt to reverse the misdeed. If we cannot undo what we have done or if too much time has passed to resolve the situation, we may try to make amends in other ways. Whether or not we can make amends, we must accept responsibility for our mistake and move on, hoping to have contained the damage as much as possible and learned from the experience.

Similarly, it is inadvisable to act out of desperation, because desperation is irrational, illogical, and impatient. When we are desperate for a certain result, we make mistakes and cut corners and usually fail to reach our goal. Desperation can lead to addictive behavior. When the emotional mind leads, it demands immediate gratification regardless of the long-term consequences. Conversely, your instincts are designed to work with the laws of Nature to protect your interests. In a spiritual sense, acting out of desperation is equivalent to selling your soul for a cause, which will never work to your advantage but always at your expense. Realistically, we need never feel desperate. We are here on this earth for a short period. If we adjust our priorities to be in tune with the realities of Nature, we will understand that nothing on this earth is worth trading our souls and our freedom for.

Vengeance is another emotion that should never motivate us to act. Vengeance, that urge to "get even" with someone who has hurt us, is uninformed by the intellect. It prompts us to cross our own ethical boundaries and encourages us to adapt an attitude that the end justifies the means. Through vengeance, we may accomplish our goals, but we pay a dear price by compromising our morals. If someone has hurt you badly but is no longer capable of inflicting harm on you or anyone else, then lick your wounds, be cautious in the future, and move forward. If, on the other hand, your enemy still remains a potent threat, you have a right and a responsibility to neutralize it. In this case, you are acting for the right reason, not out of vengeance but in self-defense. However, in planning and executing your actions, use the intellect to make sure you are acting in self-defense and that your actions never, ever cross ethical boundaries.

The principle is clear: we can accept Nature's terms, work to understand ourselves, and utilize our talents wisely to make the most of our limited time on earth, or we can attempt to live carefree, exciting lives on our own terms and hope for the best. At times, we might feel that certain rules of Nature are unfair, but Nature does not concern itself with what is fair or unfair in human terms. Rather, Nature applies the laws of cause and effect across the board without exception.

Any person who is willing to recognize Nature's fundamental rules without rationalization or sentimentality will without further effort lower the level of stress in his or her life. Although the majority of us instinctively understand the rules Nature has designated, many of us do not like them. If we want to live stress-free, we do not have the luxury of taking action based solely on our likes and dislikes. We must instead base our actions on what is in our best interest, according to Nature. For example, if Nature has provided a person with a healthy body, according to Nature, it is that person's primary duty to take good care of that body, if he expects it to serve him well. Is it difficult to understand this fundamental rule Our Maker has set before us? No. Yet many people disrespect their bodies and take their health for granted. One does not have to be a rocket scientist to understand, for example, that the lungs are designed for specific purposes—to provide oxygen to and remove toxic carbon dioxide from the blood. Yet, in spite of warning labels, people continue to smoke tobacco.

Power, prestige, and privilege are major factors that prompt people to try to manipulate Nature's ground rules, especially in the political and corporate arenas. Acts of political corruption and corporate greed are purported by the most well-educated, sophisticated, and intelligent members of society—the elite—who, in spite of their fine intellects, are leading with their emotions. They usually understand Nature's rules instinctively but choose to ignore them, perhaps because they see themselves as exempt from such moral regulations. Like others who opt for the phantom third option, they abide by the laws of Nature that appeal to them and ignore those that don't. However, the truth of the matter is that Nature dictates that we respect what it has created, including ourselves and other living beings. Sacrificing the well-being of others for one's personal gain goes strictly against Nature's laws and guarantees high levels of stress, the signal that we are not living in line with Nature's mandates. We cannot break the laws of Nature and spend life behaving just as we please and expect to come out ahead.

When we are tuned in to Nature, we invalidate stress by having the courage to face reality, the clarity to assess the threats in our particular situation, and the confidence to solve our own problems. Nature offers valuable lessons at every step of our lives. The most important lesson is that accepting Nature's mandates eliminates stress, even in an area as challenging as raising a family. If the trials of family life are taken in stride, it can be a wonderful experience. When entertaining the idea of raising a family, we need to consider many things beforehand:

1. Nature provides many possible matches for each of us. It is important that we follow our instincts and take as much time as necessary to pick a compatible partner. There is no predetermined timetable for this process.

2. In our partnerships, we must develop solid bonds through mutual

caring, mutual respect, and mutual trust before we embrace the idea of bringing children into this world. If any one of these three aspects is missing in a relationship, the partnership will likely dissolve.

3. Both partners must be willing to take on the task of raising a family before that task is begun.

4. To provide a safe, secure family environment for children, both partners must make any necessary adjustments to their lifestyles.

5. Despite good intentions and preparations, taking care of children and guiding them toward a strong and productive adulthood is an on-the-job learning experience for any parent. However, parenting is more fruitful if there is a good understanding and working relationship between parents.

Parenting, like other challenging endeavors, can feel quite stressful. As with any other area where stress appears, we must consider it a signal from Nature that we are out of line with its dictates and must choose to either change the situation or change our attitude toward it. We must also make sure to balance the instinctual, intellectual, and emotional aspects of our minds, leading with whichever one is appropriate to the situation. Parenting can feel like a minefield of stresses, because it often triggers emotional responses created during our own childhoods. Both parents must strive to recognize their own emotional triggers and make parenting decisions with the intellectual mind in the lead rather than the emotional mind.

No parent will ever be perfect, but we can be good role models for our children by illustrating how to face threats to our peace of mind with courage, clarity, and confidence. Parents who conquer stress rather than manage it give their children a head start on becoming adults who understand their strengths and limitations as well as their place in the world, according to the laws of Nature.

Smart individuals learn Nature's lessons the easy way; intelligent people learn them the hard way; and ignorant people never learn any lessons and blame the world for their misery. Learning lessons from Nature is not only a gratifying experience but also a humbling one.

*Four*

---

# The Partnership between
# Stress and Addiction

As we've determined, we are responsible as individuals for following Nature's laws, including balancing the three aspects of our minds. Our ignorance and imperfections, however, influence many to stray from the straightforward path Nature has laid out for us to indulge in destructive, habit-forming behavior. Which comes first in this match made in hell: stress or addiction? It is hard to say who leads the charge to make our lives miserable. At times, stress encourages us to numb ourselves with addictive behaviors. Other times, while seeking a momentary pleasure, thrill, or comfort, we fall into addictive habits, such as compulsive eating, smoking cigarettes or pot, drinking alcohol, snorting cocaine, or shooting heroin—behaviors that open the door to stress. Either way, the combination of stress and addiction can be completely demoralizing: together they cloud our judgment, dampen our spirits, rob us of our physical and mental health, and create ripple effects in our families. Stress and addiction feed off each other in such a way that an individual in their grip finds it hard to regain his bearings, clean up his act, and find the path to a peaceful, productive, and prosperous life.

The three most common self-inflicted problems that face affluent societies (such as the United States) are alcoholism, drug addiction, and obesity. An alcoholic might intuitively understand Nature's mandate—that he must either take responsibility for his drinking or quit drinking altogether—but he might continue to try to take that mythical third path, the one fraught with cheap excuses and rationalizations, such as the following:

- My body craves alcohol due to its genetic disposition, making it impossible for me to quit.
- I enjoy the effects of alcohol on my psyche—it is soothing, comforting, and relaxing.
- Even though I've gotten traffic tickets for driving while intoxicated and my drinking has disrupted my home life, work performance, and finances, I'm not willing to cut alcohol out of my life, but I'll try to reduce my consumption.
- Many of my friends can control their liquor consumption, so I can too.
- I lead a stressful life, and therefore I deserve a break.

Similarly, in spite of the possibility of arrest and the dangers of addiction, people consume illegal drugs, such as marijuana, heroin, methamphetamine, and crack cocaine, which harm the body and, often, the user's chances of success in the world. Why do they do this? Many people find ingesting chemicals soothing or thrilling, and they favor this instant gratification over the long-term effects these substances have on the bodies Nature gave them. People who overeat also focus on the immediate pleasure they derive from eating rather than paying attention to the effects the habit has on their physical health. Sensible eating is another fundamental rule of Our Maker. Most people understand this fact but are unwilling to follow it because it is not to their liking. These individuals are trying to have their cake and eat it too. They break the laws of Nature in an attempt to reach their goals of comfort and ease, only to end up stressed-out beyond measure. Addictive habits such as alcoholism, drug consumption, and overeating threaten the peace of mind of not only addicts but also of their loved ones, creating a ripple effect of stress.

An alcoholic who is committed to cleaning up his act must follow the laws of Nature, which dictate:

1.  Ultimately we are responsible for the stress in our lives—not our genetics or environment or other people or God.

2.  Stress is a message to us from Nature telling us to correct our outlook and behaviors. Nature accepts no excuse or rationalization for refusing to take corrective measures. It holds us responsible for our actions and dispenses consequences accordingly.

3.  In the short term, alcohol might have helped the alcoholic to manage stress by allowing him to relax, access creativity, or enjoy social situations more easily. But in return the addiction demands his soul. No one should sell his soul for any kind of benefit—mental, material, or monetary. In order to retrieve his soul, an addict must face the source of his stress with courage, clarity, and confidence.

4.  It is impossible to manage the stress of an addiction. The addict must instead conquer the addiction and the stress associated with it by *accepting* that he must give up the habit permanently. He may miss alcohol for a short period of time, but, having accepted Nature's mandate, he will never have to face strong urges to indulge in alcohol again.

5.  Nature requires that we make adjustments in our temperament, disposition, expectations, and lifestyle to overcome an addiction permanently.

6.  There is no free lunch. Nature dictates that we must give up something to get something back in life. When we give up an addiction, we are giving up the pleasure, thrill, or comfort in return for our health, peace of mind, and prosperity—in other words, a stress-free life.

7.  As no two human beings are identical, no two addicts are identical. The bond between addict and addiction is defined by the individual and not by the substance. Each alcoholic must first understand the reasons for drinking and the need to drink. What is the deep fear he is drinking to soothe? He must face that fear with courage and then design corrective measures that will suit his mental disposition and lifestyle. Only then will it be possible to renounce the addiction forever.

Similarly, the overweight among us may offer excuses and rationalizations for their problem, such as slow metabolism, time constraints, or inability to part with favorite foods. We look for shortcuts—appetite suppressants and fad diets—the first indication that our desire to maintain a healthy weight is not a commitment but wishful thinking. If we are truly committed to maintaining a healthy weight forever, the laws of Nature dictate the following:

1.  Food is primarily nutritional fuel for our bodies and not an emotional reward. Our relationship with food must be determined by the body's need for fuel rather than emotional wants. To free ourselves from stress, we must make decisions with our rational minds. While emotional satisfaction is an important part of life, the emotions cannot rule if we are to live stress-free.

2.  Ultimately, caloric balance is a simple equation between input and output. When we eat more calories than our bodies burn, we gain weight; when we eat fewer calories, we lose weight; when we eat just the right amount, we maintain our weight. We must resist turning this simple law of Nature into a complex mathematical or chemical puzzle. The hard truth is that some people burn more calories per day while others burn fewer. Through trial and error, we learn our bodies' caloric and nutritional needs. Then we are free to select the type and quantity of food that also results in emotional satisfaction.

3.  While other addicts must turn away from the chemicals to which they are addicted, a person with a food addiction must continue to eat on a daily basis. Those of us who tend to use food in ways other than as Nature intended must be vigilant and monitor why we eat, what we eat, when we eat, where we eat, and how much we eat for the rest of our lives.

    Nature also dictates that our bodies need physical activity, and exercise makes it easier to maintain a healthy weight. The bottom line is that all of us need exercise even to maintain proper weight.

4.  Managing a healthy weight has to be a daily, ongoing ritual forever for all of us, ordinary and prominent citizens alike. The sooner we embrace this concept, the sooner it will become a comfortable routine.

A CASE IN POINT: George, a thirty-six-year-old stockbroker, came to see me because of his cocaine addiction, which had created a lot of stress in his life. He came from a middle-class family. Both his parents were blue-collar workers. He was a brilliant, brash, ambitious, and cocky individual. He had had expensive tastes from a young age, and he had always known that he would have to work hard and earn a lot of money to enjoy the kind of lavish lifestyle he craved. After his graduation from business school, he became a stockbroker. He learned quickly the tricks of the trade, such as short selling and options trading. He became a mutual fund manager at a large investment firm at a young age. Between 2003 and 2006 he made a lot of money for himself and for his employers.

It was in 2005 that George felt secure in his business. He began to enjoy the life he had always wanted by going to parties, drinking alcohol, and engaging in wild sex. When he was introduced to cocaine, he found he liked the high very much. Soon he was addicted and started to smoke it instead of sniffing it. Along with the cocaine addiction came sex orgies. At the height of his addiction, George spent twenty to twenty-five thousand dollars per month entertaining himself and his friends. What started as an occasional amusement became a regular weekend routine. On weekdays George would deal with the real world, but he was always eager to enter his fantasy world on the weekends. Eventually he found the fantasy world more appealing than the real world. He lost the drive to succeed in his profession. Managing his mutual fund became a means to an end.

To manage a mega mutual fund properly, an individual must not only be mentally sharp and physically fit, but he also has to care about the people who put their trust in him to take care of their money. Once his priorities shifted, George lost his edge and a lot of money. He was let go by his employers. Stress entered his life the day he lost his job in 2008. He was not able to secure another job, as the business world was in turmoil and would be through 2009. The little savings he had evaporated quickly, but his cocaine habit persisted. He sold his fancy car and his penthouse to support it, and when that money was gone, he borrowed from wherever he could to support it. He bounced between the stress and his addiction with no end in sight. The day he asked his mother for money to pay his rent, he believed he had hit the lowest point of his life. His mother recommended him to me. In fact, she brought him to my office for the initial consultation and paid for my services.

George opted for the Turning Point Treatments. I asked him if he thought he could stay away from alcohol, cocaine, and sex for at least one month before he came for his first treatment.

He laughed and said, "Dr. Prasad, I've already been clean for the past two months, because I haven't had any money for women and drugs."

I chuckled at his statement, but I did not like his reasoning. I told him that he was arrogant, obnoxious, and self-centered. He was down in the dumps but not down on his knees. He was intelligent but not smart. He wanted to know why I thought he wasn't smart.

At his age, I told him, smart individuals did not take money from their parents to pay for rent, food, and medical services. He had failed to see how much he was hurting his mother, I told him, but I had certainly seen the pain on her face. I told him that his mother reminded me of my own mother, whom I had lost to cancer twenty-two years earlier. My mother's last words to me were that if by chance she came back to this world, she wanted me to be her son again. Twenty-two years later, her words still brought tears to my eyes. I will be honored to be her son forever. I asked George what would be his mother's last wish for him? When I said that, George's facial expression changed dramatically. Tears came to his eyes. He nodded and promised me he would change for the better. I told him to go to the waiting room and promise his mother that going forward from that day onward he would make her proud of him. When he did so, both his mother and I knew that he meant every word and that the sentiment came not from his mouth but from his heart. I knew his attitude and priorities had shifted for the better.

Over the next two months I gave George two treatments. When he visited me four months after his last treatment, he certainly was a changed man. The positive changes in his attitude, outlook, and priorities helped him put a lid on his addictions and conquer stress. He had no desire to return to his old habits. He could not explain his newfound elation and enthusiasm. He was no longer stressed. He knew he would have to work hard to put his life back in order. His first task was to pay back all the money he had borrowed from his mother. He told me that he was making progress in the business world and was confident that he would soon clear all his debts.

This case illustrates how easy it is to get into trouble or mess up your life, and how hard it is to pull out of trouble and put your life in order once again. The saying "An ounce of prevention is worth a pound of cure" definitely applies in this situation.

Some stressed-out individuals seek relief and comfort in chemical substances, and they return to these substances again and again to re-create those positive feelings. This is one of the reasons it is hard to convince stressed-out addicts to part with their addictions.

A CASE IN POINT: A forty-five-year-old woman, Janet, sought my help to quit smoking. For the past three years, she had tried to stop smoking using Chantix, Zyban, and nicotine patches, all of which had failed. Three months before she came to see me, Janet had suffered a severe bout of bronchitis for which she was hospitalized for five days. Her doctor told her that if she did not quit smoking, she would die soon due to some kind of lung ailment. She got scared and tried again to stop smoking. Again she failed. She wanted to know why she was unable to stop smoking even though she had tried hard. I told her that when it comes to addictions, you do not *try* to give them up. Either you do it or you don't. By saying that you will try, you have already lost the battle before you've even started.

I really wanted to know what was holding Janet back from quitting. I asked her to describe her relationship with the smoking habit. She confessed that she really thought of cigarettes as her lifeline. She feared that if she escaped death by giving up smoking, stress might kill her instead. She felt she could neither live with cigarettes nor without them.

As I listened, I could see that basically she was an impatient, anx-ious, and short-tempered person. She hated deadlines with a passion. Unfortunately, life is filled with deadlines. One day in college, she was overwhelmed by the amount of homework assignments she had to submit the next day. She was completely stressed-out. Meanwhile, her roommate, who had the same credit load, seemed calm and content, doing her homework with a cigarette in her mouth. Without even giving it a second thought, Janet grabbed her roommate's pack of cigarettes and smoked her first one. At first she felt dizzy, but ultimately she enjoyed the experience. Before long, cigarettes became her best friend.

Now, after years of companionship, she felt forced to abandon her best friend. She was angry at her predicament. She felt that it was unfair that she had to let go of the one thing she loved the most. Whenever she tried to quit smoking, she got agitated and angry and lashed out at everyone, both at home and at work. To keep the peace, she always went back to smoking within a day or two. She was scared that without cigarettes she would remain miserable for the rest of her life.

I gave this patient my patented speech: There are two ways, I told her, to resolve an issue that we do not like. We can either change the situation to our liking, which is easier said than done, or we can adjust ourselves to the situation. She must make up her mind to be either a comfortable smoker or a comfortable nonsmoker. At present, she was neither. I told her that she was welcome to try making smoking cigarettes into a healthy habit. But if she couldn't, she would have to come to grips with the situation and get rid of the cigarettes. If she decided to be a comfortable nonsmoker, she must let go of her best friend and have the courage to conquer her stress without cigarettes. Even with my powerful Turning Point Treatments, I told her, she would find it hard to stop smoking; therefore, she should be prepared for a tough battle ahead.

She knew that because of her health she could not be a comfortable smoker. She agreed to the treatments, and I gave her a total of two. She gave up smoking completely after the first treatment, but only with great difficulty was she able to control her anger. After the second treatment and not smoking for three months, she gave me the good news that she had neither smoked nor killed anyone. She was practicing being calm and cool, both at home and at work, and she felt that she was certainly a work in progress.

Some addicts take the perks and privileges that they enjoy for granted. They honestly believe the rules and regulations of this world and the laws of Nature do not apply to them, because that is what they've been led to believe. Eventually their reckless behavior and their arrogant and overconfident temperaments end up hurting not only them but also others around them.

A CASE IN POINT: Fred, a fifty-five-year-old successful business-man, came to my office seeking my help quitting smoking and losing fifty pounds. He was a polite, pleasant gentleman. During our consultation, Fred told me that he had tried to stop smoking and lose weight in the past and had failed. He was desperate for solutions. However, he said, he knew better than to look for an easy way out.

"I realize," he said, "that even with your help, I have my work cut out for me. I just want you to know that I'm in it for the long haul. I'm prepared to do whatever it takes."

"Good!" I replied. "You seem committed to the task. Yet you have failed in the past. I need to know what is holding you back from winning this battle."

"To be honest with you, I don't know. My good guess is that it's because I'm under a lot of stress. For the past nine months, my life has been turned upside down."

I asked Fred to give me one good reason why he wanted to stop smoking and lose weight. He told me that he wanted to live a long life. He knew that smoking alone could kill him, and adding obesity to his smoking habit only made him sure his days were numbered. He was a type-2 diabetic and took medication for that condition. His doctor had told him that if he continued to gain weight, he would have to add insulin to his regimen to control his diabetes. He also took medications for blood pressure. For the past year, he had increased his smoking from a half a pack to almost a pack a day. During that time he had also gained about thirty pounds.

"It's strange," Fred said, "but it seems like the more I try, the harder it gets. It just doesn't make sense to me. I'm not a dummy. Yet I just can't seem to break these habits. I feel really helpless. Three weeks ago, I woke up with a mild tightness in my chest. At first I thought it was just indigestion. But my wife insisted I see my doctor. He suggested that maybe I'd had a silent heart attack. But all the tests came back negative. This time I was lucky. On the way home, I thought that this episode was a wake-up call for me."

Fred thought he would finally be able to take quitting smoking and losing weight seriously. To his chagrin, however, he could not accomplish either one. He thought maybe he was using smoking and snacking to cope with stress. He wondered if he were afraid to change. He worked hard and took good care of his family. He always enjoyed smoking a few cigarettes before he went to work. In the evening, after his workday, he enjoyed a good meal, a drink, and a few cigarettes. Those were his rewards for a job well done. For the past nine months, he had been smoking more, snacking all day, and drinking more than three glasses of wine in the evening.

When I asked Fred to help me determine the cause of his stress, he responded immediately that it was his eighteen-year-old son. Although Fred worked fourteen-hour days running his business, he said he was never stressed at work. He treated his employees well, and they worked hard for him. His problems, he said, started when he came home. He had been married for twenty-five years. He loved his wife and thought she loved him too. But she was a high-strung, stubborn individual. Many times, just to keep peace in the house, Fred would go along with her. They had two children—a twenty-two-year-old daughter and an eighteen-year-old son. They loved their children, and Fred admitted that as parents they had probably been generous to a fault. Their daughter, according to Fred, had turned out "just fine." She was about to finish her education and settle into a career. But their son, Jake, was another story. Jake had always been impetuous and impatient. Fred wondered if he and his wife should have been more careful and set some strict boundaries for him from the very beginning. Fred felt his wife pampered Jake and gave in to all of his demands. "No" was a forbidden word in their house when it came to Jake.

"I made a big mistake by keeping quiet and letting my wife spoil my son," Fred said. "Now I feel guilty for not disciplining him, and I feel responsible for his bad behavior."

At fourteen, Jake had started to smoke cigarettes and drink alcohol. Two years later, he got into the habit of taking OxyContin. By seventeen, he was a heroin addict. He had been cited twice by the police for DUI. He had overdosed on heroin four months ago and had to be hospitalized. He had been on the critical list for a few days and was lucky to have survived the episode. For the past three years, he had been under the care of a psychiatrist, who had diagnosed ADHD and prescribed medication. Fred did not feel that the psychiatrist or the medication had helped his son. After Jake was discharged from the hospital, Fred and his wife enrolled him in a three-month in-patient drug rehabilitation program. They got a call three weeks later that Jake had run away from the center. With the help of police and a private investigator, Fred and his wife found Jake in a crack house with a group of other junkies, using drugs. He was returned to the rehab center. Since then, he had been begging his parents to bring him back home, promising that he would behave. Fred didn't want to do it. He didn't trust his son, but his wife insisted that they bring him home and give him a chance to prove himself.

"Now you know the source of my stress," Fred said. "I'm lost."

The first thing I told Fred was, "Stop feeling guilty. It will cloud your judgment. The fact is, you are a hardworking and caring father, but you have a problematic child. First, don't blame yourself for your son's irresponsible behavior, and second, understand that you may have to support him for the rest of your life. Once you accept these facts, you'll be at peace with yourself. Would tough love from the beginning have made a difference in your son's behavior? No one can answer that question. However, look at your daughter, who grew up in the same environment. She is just fine. Don't let your son's addictions hold you hostage. Going forward, do the right thing: take care of yourself first, and then take care of your family. Stop making excuses about why you don't straighten up your own act. If you end up in a hospital with a stroke or a heart attack, none of your excuses and explanations will come to your rescue. You have a responsibility for taking good care of your body. Do not use your body as a punching bag. Do not take your frustrations out on your body. It will certainly backfire. If your body gives up on you, you lose everything.

"Next, assert yourself at home. Set strong and sensible ground rules for your family. You have paid a lot of attention to your business and very little to your family. You allowed your wife to pamper your son. He took undue advantage of her unconditional love and turned out to be a manipulative teenage drug addict. He will continue to behave the same way as long as possible. It is high time for both of you to exercise tough love and hope that he will turn around to be a responsible young adult. If your wife really loves your son, she will cooperate with you. Tell your son that he can come home under certain conditions. Let him know that you no longer support his present lifestyle. Those days are gone for good. Tell him that you will not bail him out every time he gets into trouble with the law and drug dealers. You will provide him only the bare necessities—food, shelter, and education. He should not expect any other perks from either of you. Let him hear the forbidden word, 'no,' from both of you, and let him know that he'd better get used to it. Let him realize that the world beyond your home will not bend over backward to accommodate his needs. Such realization may prompt him to appreciate your love and concern for him.

"Tough love works wonders. More than us, animals in their natural habitat have recognized this fact. For example, the eagle instinctively knows when to stop feeding the chicks and prompt them to fend for themselves. If a chick refuses to budge, they peck the young one and push it out of the nest for its own good. If all your efforts fail to reha-bilitate your son, cut him loose, and let Nature take its course. If he is determined to ruin his life, there is nothing you can do about it. I know it is easier said than done, but at this point, you have no other choice. If you follow my advice, you will have a clear conscience forever, which in turn will set you free from stress."

Fred liked the idea of taking charge of his life. He agreed to eat healthy foods, drink alcohol only occasionally, and stop smoking for good. He would put his foot down with his wife and son. He decided that from this point on, he would operate from strength, not from weakness. To help Fred make his case to his wife, I spoke to her and explained the benefits of tough love. I urged her to cooperate with her husband if she didn't want to visit her son in prison, intensive care, or the morgue. My blunt statements shook her up, and she promised to take action to save her son from self-destruction.

I gave Fred two Turning Point Treatments to give him a head start in his quest. Three months after his second treatment, he came to my office for a follow-up visit. Since the treatments, he had felt at peace with himself. He had not smoked and felt quite comfortable as a nonsmoker.

He was eating healthy foods and not snacking as he had before. He learned to enjoy a light lunch and a decent meal in the evening. He also started to walk two miles every day. He had lost nine pounds in three months. He was confident that he could maintain these lifestyle changes and keep his weight under control for the rest of his life.

He was also happy to note that Jake was making progress in putting his life in order. The message "shape up or ship out" coming from both Fred and his wife definitely had a positive impact on Jake. He hadn't appreciated the privileges given to him by his parents but instead had taken them for granted. Once he was made aware that responsibilities and rewards go hand in hand, Jake was compelled to act like a responsible individual.

Many stressed-out individuals vent their frustrations through nervous habits, such as biting their nails, tapping their feet, or playing with their hair. These habits are classified by most mental health professionals as impulse control disorders, but I consider them addictions. Specifically, like addictions, these chemical-free habits comfort the stressed-out individual. And like addictions, these behaviors are destructive ones. These individuals, like other addicts, must trace the roots of their addictions and neutralize the stress to free them from the compulsions that lead to addictive behavior.

Some people, most of them girls and women, find it soothing when they are upset, frustrated, or bored to not just play with but actually pull out their own hair. The medical term for this condition is *trichotillomania*—"trich" or TTM for short. I have seen bald spots on scalps ranging from the size of a quarter to the palm of a hand. One patient had to wear a wig to cover her bald spot. Psychiatric journals report that some girls not only pull out their hair but also swallow it. Experts are baffled by this condition, and the cause remains unknown. Tranquilizers and antidepressants are ineffective in treating TTM, and cognitive behavior modification and group therapy have only been able to help a few of its sufferers.

I have treated ten patients for this condition, all females ranging in age from seventeen to thirty-two. Four of the ten patients came from broken homes, and the rest came from stable family environments. All of these patients could be described as sensitive, sentimental, bright idealists. They had the drive to work hard and make something out of their lives. But lack of confidence and self-esteem held them back from reaching their full potential. One patient was angry at her father for walking out of her life to marry a woman other than her mother. Another patient was upset by a difficult work relationship she felt helpless to address. Most of them had difficulty accepting that other people can be selfish, unethical, rude, and inconsiderate. The main source of their stress was that they could not seem to accept the world as it is and work with it on its terms.

If I could be of any help to them, I knew that one question needed to be answered. Why would only a handful of people among all the stressed-out individuals in the world resort to pulling out their hair as a coping mechanism? When I asked my patients why they did it, all of them told me that they got a pleasant tingling sensation instead of pain when they pulled their hair out by the roots. What started as a random nervous habit became a pleasurable pastime, a relief from the stress they were feeling. Based on the fact that these people feel a pleasant sensation when others feel pain leads me to believe that the habit is caused by an anomaly in the hardwiring of the brain. Naturally, one cannot change that. But certainly it is possible to change the outlook and attitude of an individual to make the adjustments necessary to deal with this condition.

My Turning Point Program, including treatments, helped my patients with TTM to become less sensitive and idealistic and more sensible and realistic. All of these patients are doing well. They have adjusted to this imperfect world. While they haven't completely stopped pulling out their hair, none of them have bald patches anymore. One patient who wore a wig was able to discard it within a few months after the treatments.

Stress and addiction go hand in hand, equal partners in crime. When they work together, they feed each other like fuel feeds a fire, and they can easily explode in your face. However, don't forget that you have created the stress and addictions in your life, and therefore Nature expects you to dispense of them. It is your choice to allow them to control your life or to stand up and be the master of your own destiny. If smoking, drinking, overeating, or taking drugs could solve your problems and free you from stress in the long term, I would be the first one to advise you to be addicted to all of them. But what can really free you from stress is tuning into Nature and allowing it to guide you off that destructive path.

Nature's essential message is clear: in this complex and complicated world, we can drum up excuses and rationalizations for refusing to take charge of our lives and as a result struggle needlessly and to no good end, or we can choose to look rationally and honestly at what Nature requires of us and as a result enjoy our short passage on this planet. Nature gives each of us gifts, but what we make of those gifts is up to us. You can choose to be your own best friend or your own worst enemy. All your strength must come from within, because no external source can provide it. Nature has created you with all the strength you need. Now you must learn to believe in yourself and confidently make your place in the world.

---

# Five

# Understanding Yourself and Your Place in the World

Failure to reach goals, make good on promises, and take advantage of opportunities are a few of the many reasons we feel stress. Fortunately, no matter how disappointing life has been thus far, reversing the tide and leading a stress-free life is not difficult if you commit to working with Nature rather than against it. Working with Nature means taking a realistic look at yourself and where you might fit in the world. Nature has given us three divisions of the mind, and we must take all three into consideration when making a decision or taking action. When we follow the laws of Nature as diligently as we can, the results serve the best interests of everyone involved. We know we've made a decision in line with Nature's laws when that decision diffuses rather than increases a feeling of stress.

The instinctual, intellectual, and emotional aspects of our minds affect at least five sectors of our lives: the physical, the professional, the personal, the financial, and the social. We have certain responsibilities defined by Nature in each of these sectors. As you inventory these sectors in the pages that follow, remember that your impressions of yourself are likely to be biased in some areas. When you suspect that your perspective is skewed, either positively or negatively, ask wise friends, trusted family members, and, if necessary, mental health professionals to share their perspectives with you. Above all, you want to see yourself with clarity. However, in the end the final assessment of yourself, your priorities, and your expectations must be your own. This task cannot be delegated to anyone else. Having an accurate picture of yourself is crucial if you intend to conquer stress for good.

In examining these areas of our lives, it is incumbent upon each of us to recognize their relative significance. Part of our mission is to manage and balance the various sectors appropriately, in our best interest. Unfortunately, few of us are sensible and humble enough to keep all the sectors of our lives balanced. Success in one or two sectors often goes to our heads, and, leading with our emotions, we assume that these strong sectors can offset the other, weaker sectors and carry us forward without a hitch. Look at Charlie Sheen, a talented actor who was carried away by his professional success and as a result neglected the personal sector of his life and eventually lost his contract, his credibility, and his reputation. His actions, spurred by his emotional mind and a misguided attempt at self-defense, also negatively affected his family and the people with whom he worked. Such an unbalanced approach to life is shortsighted and unrealistic. Even physicians, lawyers, scientists, and engineers, who are successful by virtue of their intellectual talents rather than their physical attributes, have to pay attention to the physical sector of their lives in order to protect their health and sanity. And all of us must balance the three aspects of our minds and remember our connection to Nature, Our Maker.

## THE PHYSICAL SECTOR

Begin your self-evaluation with the physical sector, which includes your appearance and your biological health. First, consider your appearance. Stand in front of a mirror and take a good, hard look at yourself. If you are lucky, the image you see is appealing. If you see nothing attractive about your reflection, first consider that your expectations might be unrealistic. Nature endows each of us with gifts. Even if you cannot approve fully of what you see in the mirror, accept what Our Maker has given you to work with. Tell yourself that from now on you will respect your body's strengths and tolerate its shortcomings.

Then proceed to improve upon those aspects of your appearance that you might improve upon without harming yourself in any way, for example, switching from wearing eyeglasses to wearing contact lenses. Consider your clothing and your hair. Which styles feel most comfortable to you? Have you gotten compliments from people you trust and admire about a certain haircut or certain items of clothing? Don't concern yourself with what people you don't trust or admire say about your looks. They might have ulterior motives in commenting about your appearance. Comfort with the appearance Nature has given you leads to freedom and self-confidence.

Nature blesses some of us with physical traits that match the ideals of beauty in our culture. These people, if so inclined, might make use of this gift by pursuing careers in show business, modeling, politics, or other professions where appearance is a crucial element. Obviously, appearance will be more important to this population than to, say, physicians or scientists, who most likely value intellect more than appearance. People who make a living in part by their appearance invest more time and money in this area than the average person. But those who are naturally beautiful must also cultivate the talents located in other aspects of their lives—especially the spiritual, emotional, and financial sectors—if they seek long-term peace of mind. In our current culture, which exalts a youthful appearance, popularity based on looks alone will not last. Once they retire or lose popularity, many public figures become depressed and socially isolated.

If you have been born with disabling physical attributes, understand and accept that these attributes are no fault of your own. All of our attributes are simply a reality of life. Resentment over any shortcoming, real or imagined, can only make life more difficult. Capitalize on whatever physical strengths you might have, and whenever possible and appropriate, take advantage of the sophisticated technology that might be available to mitigate your disability.

Any person fixated on physical appearance can experience stress associated with that sector of life. Some people, whether they feel they are uglier or more beautiful than average, become anxious and self-conscious in public settings. These feelings might encourage a person to isolate herself from the world by avoiding social settings or insulate himself from the world by using alcohol or other chemicals to soothe insecurities. Such a chain reaction is triggered by a *vanity complex*, the irrational concern with physical appearance, which can transform a person into a socially awkward, professionally inadequate, sexually inhibited, and spiritually deprived individual. This path is not what Nature has in mind.

People who struggle with a vanity complex are giving their emotional minds too much headway and ignoring the input of their instinctual and intellectual minds. Instincts tell us, for example, that different people are attracted to different physical attributes, while the intellect reminds us that physical attributes are supplemented by personality traits that can increase attractiveness. Acknowledging and accepting the physical body Nature has given you is an indispensable step in the quest for a stress-free life.

Next, evaluate your biological health, the proper functioning of your body's organs and systems. The human body is an amazing, durable piece of machinery, aptly designed by Nature to meet its obligations. As I've mentioned, we must take good care of our bodies if we expect them to serve us well. Don't overlook the nutritional aspects and physical activities that are vital to maintaining your health.

Those of us who have biological health issues, for example diabetes, must pay more attention to this sector and adjust our lives accordingly, whether that means monitoring our diets, exercising, or learning how to maintain normal blood-sugar levels. Anyone with chronic health problems, no matter how successful he is professionally and financially, must manage this sector carefully, or it will cause his downfall. Good health occurs only when we appreciate the bodies with which we have been blessed and never take them for granted, regardless of what we perceive as our shortcomings. Regardless of what Nature has given us, we are obligated to be the best we can be.

## THE PROFESSIONAL SECTOR:

This is the "bread-and-butter" sector, which, if managed well, helps you earn a living. This sector is prone to stress, because we live in an extremely competitive world and we are not always honest with ourselves about our professional strengths and weaknesses. We must be honest, vigilant, innovative, thoughtful, and proactive in order to be successful professionally. None of us can earn a decent living on our own terms; it has to be done on mutually beneficial terms with the world.

To manage this sector efficiently and without stress, we must follow several basic guidelines. Without exception, they apply to everyone, from all walks of life, who wants or needs to work for a living. First of all, the world is a marketplace, and you are marketing your skills and talents, hoping for the opportunity to exchange these things for the money that will allow you to live comfortably and securely. It is necessary, therefore, to evaluate your God-given marketable assets in relation to the needs of this world at this point in time. You may seek feedback from the people you trust or a trained career counselor, but in the end you must conduct the final assessment of how best to make a living. This process often includes stripping away our emotional attachments to certain professions. Perhaps you've always dreamed of being a fashion designer, for example, but you know instinctively that you are a terrible artist. We must be willing to honestly assess the talents that might help us earn a living in this world. Be objective in your evaluation, as it is your responsibility to find a profession that will satisfy you.

Each of your professional strengths can apply to many different occupations. For instance, if you are a good orator, you might become a motivational speaker, a politician, or a litigation attorney. If you are an intelligent but shy person, you might work behind the scenes as a research scientist, a computer programmer, or a graphic artist. If you have people skills, you might decide to be a teacher, a doctor, or a public relations specialist. If you are the adventurous athletic type, you might try to become a professional athlete in the sport of your choice or choose to join the armed services. If you have a taste for fine cuisine, you might be a restaurant critic or train to be a chef and work toward opening your own restaurant. If formal education is a weakness for you and you decide not to go to college, you can still make a decent living working in a trade, such as a mechanic, construction worker, or farmer. There are countless opportunities for diligent, hard-working, and honest individuals to earn a decent living.

Also consider where the types of jobs you're interested in are located and whether those locations suit your strengths. Most jobs are located in cities, where the cost of living is high. The irony is that it is easy to find a job in a big city but tough to find decent and affordable housing. Weigh the costs of living in a city against those of living in a suburb. Consider that the cost of commuting from the suburbs is going up faster than one can imagine. Also consider that peak-hour traffic jams, crowded public transportation, and unpredictable weather conditions will cut into downtime or quality family time.

If you are single, a studio apartment or a one-bedroom apartment close to your workplace is better than a spacious suburban apartment. While you may cut down on expenses if you share an apartment with a roommate, it may not be a good idea, because it curtails your freedom. If you have a family, choose a smaller house closer to your workplace rather than a larger house in the suburbs to reduce your commute and increase the time you are able to spend with your family. If you choose to live a substantial distance from your workplace, do so only if you can telecommute at least part of the time. Before you accept a job offer, consider your professional strengths and weaknesses, the balance in the sectors of your life, the work environment, and where you plan to reside. Make the choices that decrease the overall amount of stress in your life.

You must believe in your professional mission and your professional agenda, and you must trust your instincts. Recognize that talent alone is not enough to guarantee work in your chosen field. When your innate talent coincides with what you love to do, you will easily sharpen that talent into a marketable tool. Sometimes, you must work hard to develop your talent and your professional connections so that you stand out in a particularly competitive field.

Unfortunately, Nature sometimes gives us intellectual talents and emotional interests that do not match, which can be a major source of stress. In this case, we must call on the intellect, instincts, and emotions to work together to find a solution. Consider, for example, a person who dreams of being an accomplished musician but is born with little or no musical talent. Instead, she has the mechanical talent to become a good engineer. This person has at least three choices:

A: She can accept the disparity between her talent and her passion, and pursue a career in engineering. However, she must accept the risk that she might never rejoice in her achievements as an engineer, because her heart is not in it.

B: She can ignore her lack of natural talent and pursue her passion for music. But she must be prepared for disappointment, since it is likely she will not reach her professional goals. This option may make her slightly unhappy professionally, and she may struggle financially, but she may also be at peace with herself and her choice.

C: She can struggle with and agonize over the cards Nature has dealt her and live feeling trapped and without a purpose in life.

The most prudent way for her to handle this dilemma would be to utilize both her talents and her passion to build an engineering career in an area related to music, such as a designer of acoustic tiles or an employee for a company that manufactures musical instruments. Simultaneously, she can pursue her musical passion as a hobby and accept whatever level of musical proficiency she attains. In this scenario, she accepts and utilizes the strengths Nature has provided rather than pursuing a pipe dream or becoming crippled by her shortcomings. Living with constant internal conflict causes stress, which in turn saps our physical, mental, and spiritual energy. It is imperative that we resolve any internal conflict between our strengths and weaknesses, our passions and priorities, if we intend to be the best we can be and make the most out of life. Resolving internal conflict means simply accepting what Nature has given us and creating a professional plan that serves our intellectual talents and our emotional needs.

Whatever professional choices you make, the task you undertake—however big or small—must be important to you. You must be willing and able to put your mind, your heart, and your soul into your work. You must feel good about yourself professionally and be proud for the right reasons—namely that you are helping to build a better world for others while also making a living for yourself. Lots of hard work, time, patience, and perseverance are needed to build a solid professional reputation. It takes one misstep and little time to turn it to dust. You are much more likely to build a good reputation if you care deeply about what you do each day.

Once you have begun to build a career in your chosen profession, the most important advice I can give you is to keep your mind, eyes, and ears open and your mouth shut. As a physician, I learned to follow this advice a long time ago. I found that if I listened carefully to my patients with an open mind and resisted the urge to interrupt them, they would give me clues that would in turn help me diagnose and treat their ailments. Even today when I diagnose, I rely more on my patient's history, physical signs, and symptoms rather than on the wide array of sophisticated gadgets I have at my disposal.

Nature dictates that you do your job to the best of your abilities. In your chosen field, look for ways to capitalize on your strengths and compensate for your weaknesses. If other people work for you, never ask them to do anything you have not demanded of yourself. Command respect and loyalty from your colleagues by treating them with consideration. Be a caring, compassionate, and good-hearted human being, and these traits will show through in every aspect of your life. However, make clear that your goodness is not a weakness. Do not allow your employer to take advantage of you, and if you are a manager, discipline employees when the situation calls for it, without ever insulting them or treating them badly. Be willing to safeguard your professional integrity at any cost. We live in an imperfect world, one in which it is tempting to lie for professional gain, but Nature's laws of cause and effect dictate that the lies that give you an initial advantage will catch up with you and cause your downfall.

Among your professional colleagues, contacts, and acquaintances, it is important to know whom to trust and not to trust. An individual is untrustworthy until he or she proves otherwise, for trust must be earned. Don't trust yes-men, because anyone who agrees with you automatically without ever questioning the veracity of your statements is most likely either dishonest or stupid. When you do find people you trust, form a tight-knit inner circle to support or carry out your professional agenda. And remember that trust is a two-way street. You must also behave in a way that will win your colleagues' or your employees' trust. Mutual trust is one factor that contributes to a low-stress work environment.

Mixing business with pleasure, however, can only lead to stress, as the two sectors run according to different agendas. In business, you are out to provide a quality product or service, make a profit via savvy negotiation, and act in your own best interest. By definition, the business environment is a formal arena. It is typically a civil environment but can also be adversarial and cold. While socializing can be a part of business, it is a mistake to develop a personal relationship with a business acquaintance for the sake of pleasure. A conflict of interest arises when a personal relationship influences a professional one, since a business transaction requires objectivity, and a personal relationship requires emotional bias.

For example, Tim, a manufacturer, built a successful and reputed business over time. He drove a hard bargain with his suppliers and delivered quality goods to his clients on time. He met Sara, a charming, articulate, and intelligent buyer for a large chain of department stores, when she visited him in his office. After a tough negotiation, they agreed to do business on mutually beneficial terms. Tim took her out to lunch at an expensive restaurant to show his appreciation, and they found they got along well. However, Tim formed a habit of taking Sara out to dinner whenever she was in town, not because it was necessary for business but because he enjoyed her company. Soon their business relationship turned into friendship.

A few months later, as a result of rising energy and health-care costs, Tim made the difficult decision to raise his prices. Sarah objected to the change, because she was unwilling to bear the extra costs or pass them on to her customers. In fact, she suggested that Tim reduce his prices because of the downturn in the economy. Their agendas clashed, and they were unable to reach an agreement. Tim felt hurt because Sara was unsympathetic to his situation, and Sara was upset that Tim was treating her like any other client in spite of their friendship. Finally, Tim stopped doing business with Sara. He regretted ever having mixed business with pleasure.

The boundary between a business relationship and a personal relationship must remain clear at all times. If you choose to do business with close friends or relatives, understand that your personal relationship may suffer as a result.

A CASE IN POINT: Evelyn, a forty-five-year-old happily married woman with two children, sought my help to quit smoking. She had picked up the habit in her early twenties and had smoked a pack a day for years. She had stopped smoking seven years before with the help of Nicorette gum to protect her health and be a good role model for her children. In the process, she gained a few pounds but got her weight under control with diet and exercise. After being a nonsmoker for six years, she started to smoke again. After a few months, she tried to quit again using Nicorette gum, a nicotine patch, and acupuncture, but none of these aids helped her stop, and she regretted going back to smoking. Evelyn had a happy home life and had no financial problems. She appeared to be an intelligent but anxious and sentimental individual. I wanted to know why she had gone back to smoking and was now unable to stop. She said that she had been under a lot of stress for the past year, and that it had made her go back to smoking. I told her that if she wanted to be a comfortable nonsmoker, she must trace the source of her stress and neutralize it.

After a long consultation, I concluded that her work was the source of her stress. Years before, she had given up her work as an interior decorator to be a full-time mom. Once her two children were grown up and independent, she decided to go back to interior decorating. She talked about it with her neighbor, Linda, a retired mid-level Wall Street executive. She too had been a stay-at-home mom, and she and Evelyn had become good friends over the years. Linda's children were also grown, and Linda expressed an interest in starting a business. They talked about starting a business together, in which Evelyn's artistic talents and Linda's Wall Street experience would be a perfect fit. They decided to invest time and money to open an interior decorating agency.

Unfortunately, after a few months, it turned out not to be such a perfect fit after all. Evelyn was a patient, sensitive, and sentimental person, whereas Linda was an impatient, insensitive, and demanding individual. The personality clash between the two became obvious immediately once they began working together. In a social setting, Evelyn had never noticed this side of Linda's behavior. But in a professional setting where the stakes were high, money was involved, and they were forced to spend long hours working together, Evelyn recognized Linda's mean streak and became unhappy with the arrangement. One day when Linda came down hard on an employee, Evelyn tried to intercede. Linda snapped at Evelyn and asked her not to interfere in business decisions and running the office. Evelyn was deeply hurt, because she felt that Linda had treated her like an employee rather than a partner.

Through this experience, Evelyn discovered that she liked Linda as a friend but not as a business partner. She agonized over whether to continue or end the partnership with Linda, and it was while agonizing that she picked up a cigarette after a six-year hiatus. I told Evelyn that the day Linda had snapped at her, she broke not only Evelyn's heart but also their friendship. I suggested that if working with Linda made good business sense, Evelyn should ignore Linda's personality and continue the partnership. If working with Linda did not make good business sense, I suggested that Evelyn dissolve the partnership. Until she made that decision, she would not be able to stop smoking. I advised her to go home and think about it. One week later Evelyn called to inform me that she had decided to dissolve their partnership. It was not difficult for her to stop smoking once this burden had been lifted.

People are sometimes drawn into financial transactions with close relatives out of a feeling of obligation. I believe that helping your parents or your children deal with financial hardships is one's duty and responsibility. However, even in these cases it is essential to recognize your financial capacity and stay within those limits. For example, when a relative asks you to cosign a loan to buy a house or car or to start a new business, think carefully before you agree. Understand that there is a possibility that they will fail to make the loan payments and that if they do so, their loan obligation becomes your responsibility. If you have worked hard to create good credit, cosigning a loan or letting someone else use your credit card can only jeopardize your own financial standing and security. If you choose to lend money to a relative, you must discuss and document the terms of the loan in writing, to be dated and signed by both parties. Even so, it is wise when lending money to a relative to consider it a gift and to prepare to lose the principal. Such a mind-set will prevent you from lending more than you can afford to lose. Then if you are repaid in full, you can be pleasantly surprised.

When you decide to lend money to a friend or family member, you enter into a separate business relationship with that person. If you want to gauge the probability of that person repaying the loan, evaluate his or her attitude, temperament, and outlook from a business point of view. Listen to your instincts, but also understand that despite all your precautions, you may still be shortchanged. If so, accept it, and move on.

Finally, if you experience professional success, do not let it go to your head. Continue to carefully balance the professional sector with the other sectors of your life in accordance with Nature's laws. Always keep in mind the valuable contributions from the other sectors in your life as well as the necessary balance between the three aspects of your mind in all sectors.

A CASE IN POINT: Bill, a corporate attorney who specialized in acquisitions and mergers, came to see me wanting to end his addiction to alcohol. He was hard-working, bright, confident, and arrogant. He had been married for thirteen years and had two sons, aged seven and five. He loved his children and tried to be part of their lives, despite his busy schedule. When he had graduated from law school, he had charted his professional career in his mind and followed his plan to a tee. Twelve years later, he had three offices—one in New York City, one in Washington DC, and one in Los Angeles—seventy-five associates, and hundreds of staff members. He knew how to build a successful business by merging politics, business, and legal ramifications. Being a savvy power broker, an eloquent orator, and a knowledgeable operator, he had earned the trust and confidence of his clients. He threw lavish parties to develop a powerful professional network. But when he came to see me, he was under lot of stress because his finances, business, and relationship with his children were all in jeopardy.

While building his business, Bill had rarely drunk alcohol. However, when his professional and financial sectors were finally secure, he started to drink more often with friends and colleagues in a social setting. As he became more successful, he enjoyed this downtime away from his strenuous work schedule and believed that he had earned the privilege to unwind. Soon his unwinding began to include extramarital affairs. He began to enjoy the social and personal aspects of his life more than managing his business. He started delegating important decisions to his associates. He became a binge drinker and, cited with three traffic tickets for driving under the influence of alcohol, lost his license. Then Bill's wife filed for divorce and demanded custody of their children. Then he made several business miscalculations and lost a large amount of money and credibility with his clients. In response to the stress from the personal sector and the professional sector, he drank more. He was desperate, he told me. He needed my help to bring sanity to his life.

Straightforward as I am, I told him that no one is above the laws of Nature, and he was defying those laws. There were no quick fixes and easy solutions for his problem. He would have to start all over to reinvent himself, guided by noble goals, insight, and pragmatic expectations. He should aspire to be a wise man, not just a bright individual. Wise men are not only master strategists and tacticians, but they are also adept at balancing the various sectors to enjoy productive and peaceful lives.

Bill's objective had been flawed in the first place: he had wanted to build an empire so that he might rake in huge profits and lead a carefree, lavish life. He had followed his instincts in choosing a profession in which he was naturally talented, and he had worked hard to make himself a star in his field. However, a wise man would have aimed to use his God-given talents and opportunities to create financial security for his family while also providing an important service to his clients and decent employment for scores of people. Such noble objectives would have earned Bill a successful and stress-free life.

I told Bill that he was battling on too many fronts and losing out big on all of them. He would have to address one issue at a time. First, he should straighten out his personal life by ending his fight in divorce court to retain custody of his children. He had betrayed the trust of his family and would have to own up to his mistakes. The longer he fought for custody, the harder it would be for the children. Therefore, he should amicably resolve his divorce to keep peace in the family.

Next, I told him that he must stop drinking alcohol and taking sleep aids and antidepressants. He needed a clear mind to navigate the grueling process of rebuilding his life. He had to pay attention to his physical health by exercising on a regular basis and eating healthy foods. The endorphins that he would generate from physical activity and the absence of alcohol and other medications would help him see the issues clearly and enable him to take appropriate actions. He agreed to all my conditions.

The Turning Point Treatment gave him a head start by mellowing his arrogance and neutralizing his urge to drink. Two years after his last treatment, he called to say that he was free of alcohol and other prescription medication. His children had forgiven him for his past behavior and were on good terms with him. He had had to make many adjustments in his professional life, but he felt he once again had control over his career.

Building a career on a faulty foundation, such as greed or arrogance, can only lead to major stress, either in the professional sector or in other sectors of life. Remain humble and keep the aspects of your mind and the other sectors of your life in sight and balanced, even at the height of your career.

## THE PERSONAL SECTOR

This area of our lives includes our personal habits and hobbies and our relationships with family and friends. In a balanced life, we carve out some time for ourselves and our own interests while also maintaining healthy relationships with the people we care about.

Anything you do or say repeatedly registers in your instinctual mind as a habit. We perform habits automatically, without thinking consciously about what we're doing. We rely on our habits, as we lead complex lives. We can comfortably ride a bicycle or drive a car while carrying on a conversation with a companion, for example, or do dishes while thinking about a work project.

The type of habit determines the impact it has on our lives. Some habits—such as being tidy, on time, or driving a car—have a positive impact, while other habits—such as being sloppy or habitually late and addictions such as drinking, smoking, and doing drugs—have a negative impact. Habits are worth considering analytically. Are your habits in line with Nature's laws? The habits that cause you stress are the ones that are not in line with Nature. One bad habit can certainly make your life miserable.

Hobbies are powerful antidotes to stress. All of us need a little break from our routine. Reading, painting, gardening, flower arranging, philanthropic work, and sports such as golf and skiing are just a few examples of hobbies that many people enjoy. My wife and I love gardening. In the spring we take a break from our daily routine and plant colorful annuals and perennials. We chat while designing our garden and then enjoy a glass of cool lemonade. At the end of the day, we both feel invigorated and relaxed. We beam with pride when our neighbors admire our garden. Hobbies are the perfect place to indulge an interest or a passion in an area in which Nature has not necessarily bestowed its greatest gifts. Hobbies recharge our batteries, lift our spirits, and help us reconnect with ourselves when we feel lost.

A CASE IN POINT: Ralph, a fifty-six-year-old recently retired police officer, happily married and financially secure, came to see me because he felt persistently agitated and couldn't sleep. His wife worked as an office manager in a law firm. Of his three children, his eldest son had just joined the police force, and the younger two were still in college. He had been a police captain before he retired and had worked long hours all his life, although he had for many years played golf occasionally for fun. Since his retirement, he had been restless and bored, although he did not feel like working full-time or part-time. So he decided to play golf full-time to occupy himself, but it didn't help. He still felt a lack of purpose in his life and experienced the sense of a deep void in his chest.

Upon his doctor's recommendation, Ralph tried sleep aids and antidepressants. Three weeks later, he stopped taking the medications, because they didn't help. I was his last hope. During our initial consultation, he told me that he loved to collect and refurbish old leather golf bags and wooden golf clubs. I seized on the detail and told him that this hobby would be the cure for his ills. I suggested he start a business to refurbish antique golf equipment, and he liked the idea very much. A year later he called me in good spirits. Once he had started his new business, his emotional problems had disappeared. He now attended major golf tournaments, where he sold refurbished bags and clubs and also met famous golf players. Fortunately for Ralph, his hobby helped him to find a new niche and a sense of purpose in life after retirement.

As parents, we should encourage our children to take up hobbies in whatever areas are of particular interest to them. Children benefit from hobbies in the same way adults do, with the added benefit of exploring potential careers with pleasure as the goal.

The personal sector also includes our relationships with our family members and friends. Take an inventory of your relationship with your parents, spouse, children, siblings, and friends. If the bond you have with these people is strong and based on a sense of mutual caring, then it is relatively easy to manage this sector well. On the other hand, suppose you don't have a good relationship with your parents. If this is true, the fault may lie with them, with you, or with both parties. If you feel that it is difficult to interact with your parents because they are selfish and irresponsible, then maintain as cordial a relationship as possible with them, without expecting much. However, if the fault lies with you, address your attitude and outlook and take corrective action immediately.

In general, the guideline for living stress-free is to keep people close who make you feel comfortable and stay clear of people who make you uncomfortable. You may never puzzle out why some people annoy you, and the reasons are ultimately irrelevant. You need never disclose your feelings to these people anyway. It is better for you if they know less about what is on your mind. My mother told me a long time ago that the best policy for staying out of trouble is to keep your mouth shut and your eyes and ears open. As a general rule, be careful to whom you disclose your feelings or intentions. This information may be used against you. Disclose your inner thoughts only when necessary and to people you trust the most. I have drawn a circle of trust around me with the people I trust most inside it. If you have even one person inside your circle, consider yourself lucky that you have a confidant and thus will never feel alone.

Some successful professionals tend to neglect the personal sector, causing stress at home or in the extended family. For instance, a professional man who takes his spouse for granted or treats her badly risks having a miserable home life. The tension between the couple will in turn have a starkly negative emotional impact on their children. Many of my patients are professionally successful individuals who fall victim to various addictions because they have made messes of their personal lives.

If you are relatively young and are honest enough to admit that you care more about career than family, you should not marry and have a family at this time. You should instead enjoy the freedom of single life and focus on professional and social development. It is important, however, that you consider whether one of your life goals is to have a spouse and a family at some point in the future. Some single professionals as they reach middle age decide that they are lonely and have nothing to look forward to. As a grandfather, I can tell you nothing beats the pleasure I get from playing with my ten-year-old grandson. Some people, however, have fulfilling lives that do not include children or even spouses. They simply have more time and energy to devote to other aspects of their personal lives. If you are uncertain whether you want a family, try to ignore the cultural beliefs that exalt marriage and parenthood. Instead, tune in to Nature. Will the gifts Nature has given you be of good use in developing an intimate relationship and raising children?

If career and family are of equal importance to you, it is possible to balance a successful professional career with a pleasant personal life. A professional woman who also wants a family may have to put her professional aspirations on hold or tone them down temporarily until the children have been born and have grown to be relatively independent. While she may during those years lose out on some advantages in the professional sector, she might consider that loss an acceptable compromise. Professional men have, by virtue of their gender, certain distinct advantages over women in the professional sector—namely because they cannot get pregnant. With that advantage comes an obligation to understand the plight of female professionals, whether they are wives or colleagues, and to extend cooperation to help these women fulfill their responsibilities. A professional man should also contribute to the care of his own children and do his part on the domestic front so that his wife is able to balance the professional and personal sectors in the same way he does.

## THE FINANCIAL SECTOR

If your finances are in line with Nature's principles, you have at least enough money to cover your financial responsibilities and a little extra to set aside for emergencies. This is called living within your means. Financial matters are relatively straightforward in that they are a zero-sum game: there is a specific amount of money to go around, and when it's gone, it's gone. It is not a good idea to depend on credit for things other than big-ticket items, such as a home and a car, because being overextended in any sector of your life puts you out of balance. Living within your means allows you to be flexible and to roll with the punches life is certain to dole out. The value of your assets changes with the economic tide, whereas the value of your liabilities remains constant until they are paid off. For example, whether you lose your job or the market value of your house declines, you still have to pay your mortgage, car loan, and utility bills.

Begin your assessment of your financial sector by distinguishing between your needs and your wants. They are not the same. Needs are items necessary for your survival. They are determined by the instincts and the intellect and are based on logic and facts. For example, when our bodies feel hunger, we eat. Eating is a need. The purpose of our homes is to shelter us from the elements. Wants, on the other hand, are optional luxury items that please us in one way or another, often by giving us a certain social status. Wants are based on emotions, and they are infinite. Once you fulfill one desire, another pops up to take its place. Trying to keep up with the Joneses is a task motivated by emotions and one that, if you give in to the impulse, will stretch into infinity.

Wants can be a main source of stress. For example, those of us who work farther than walking distance from our homes need convenient transportation to commute between home and work. If public transportation is not available, a reliable and affordable automobile will do the job. If an individual chooses an expensive sports car instead, he or she has fulfilled a want, not a need. If the sports car is more expensive than the buyer can afford, it causes an imbalance in the financial sector and a nagging feeling of stress. When we spend more than we can afford on an item, it is usually because we have made the decision with our emotions alone, rather than seeking the input of the intellect and the instincts. The gold standard of the financial sector is learning to live within your means.

A CASE IN POINT: A prominent surgeon, a colleague of mine, was married to a beautiful woman with expensive taste and a flare for opulence. By the time I got acquainted with him, he had been in practice for almost ten years. My impression of him was that he was a hard-working, ambitious, and high-strung individual. Through the grapevine, I heard that he had built a ten-thousand-square-foot house with an indoor swimming pool and a tennis court, costing him millions of dollars. His wife was an active socialite in town who wore only designer clothing. Often I wondered how as a physician he could live the luxurious life of a hedge fund manager. I thought either he had been born rich or had extra income from some other source.

A few years later, I met him one day in the doctor's lounge. He appeared to be sad and distressed. I asked him with some hesitation if something was bothering him. If so, I said, maybe I could be of some help. He looked around and made sure there was no one else in the room, and then he burst into tears. He eventually calmed down and told me that he was ruined financially and professionally. I was stunned by his confession. He explained that he was working harder now than ever before but still had fallen behind on his mortgage payments, taxes, and other financial obligations. He had maxed out all his credit sources. He had just received a notice of foreclosure from the bank on his house and his medical office. Additionally, he had lost two major malpractice suits, which had prompted his insurance company to cancel his coverage for good. He no longer could practice his specialty. Watching his empire collapse had stressed him a great deal. To top it all off, his marriage was in jeopardy because he could no longer support his wife's lavish lifestyle. A few weeks later, I heard that his house had been repossessed by the bank and that he had left town.

His story made me reflect on my own marriage. I have been married to my wife for forty-three years, and I have yet to find a reason to complain about her. In fact, she is the reason I lead a stress-free life. I was twenty-three and she was eighteen when we married. It was love at first sight for both of us. I was just out of medical school and halfway through my rotating internship. In India at that time my salary was the equivalent of fifty dollars per month. It was not even sufficient for me to buy my lunch every day. Fortunately for me, my father was a cardiologist and a good provider, and I was able to borrow money from him for my expenses. My wife came from a wealthy family, and her wealth was of some concern to me. I was worried about whether I could provide the comforts she was used to.

At the time of our marriage, she was completing her final year of college, and she continued to live at home with her parents while she finished school and I finished my internship. We lived only one mile away from each other and met quite often. About three weeks after our marriage, I got a call from her requesting that I take her out to a movie and dinner. She wanted to see the James Bond movie *From Russia with Love*. I was more than happy to accommodate her. But when I got dressed, I found that I had only three dollars in my wallet. I needed at least twenty dollars for the movie and dinner. I was about to ask my dad for money, as usual, but something made me stop short. I was no longer a bachelor. I was now a married man. It was my responsibility to take care of my wife and her needs. I could not ask my dad for money. I was caught in a dilemma. I did not know how to tell my wife that I had no money to take her out. I was afraid that she would never again respect me. But I did not want my marriage to be based on false pretenses. I decided to tell her the truth about my predicament and take my chances.

When I went to her house, she was fabulously dressed for the occasion, and she welcomed me with open arms. I explained to her my problem. It took her just two seconds to digest the information, and then she told me that I had done the right thing. I almost got tears in my eyes. She said that nothing had been lost and that we could go to the park nearby and spend a few hours together there. We went to the park and bought a bag of peanuts and a Coke. During the three hours that we spent there, just talking, we came to understand each other's sentiments very well. Afterward, we felt we had known each other for a long time. Forty-two years later, we still smile at each other and enjoy each other's company. Since then we have both always lived within our means, and together we live a stress-free, happy life. Maybe one must be lucky to find such an understanding life partner, but it is also up to each one of us to be honest with a prospective partner and find out if we are compatible financially.

## THE SOCIAL SECTOR:

This sector offers an opportunity to simply have fun as well as to develop a public persona, an aspect of ourselves that is different from the personal or professional selves that dominate the other sectors of our lives. Social settings offer us the chance to seek out entertainment and enjoy the company of other people. They provide a diversion from the demands of work and familial obligations. The best type of social gathering encourages us to speak freely and express our opinions and to learn what others think and feel about the issues that interest us, as well as learn about new issues important to the people we are with, whether our family members, friends, colleagues, or acquaintances. If managed properly, the social sector adds value to our lives. The social sector can overlap and enhance other sectors. For example, a social round of golf with colleagues or clients allows us to get some exercise outdoors while also bonding socially and professionally. Those who are married and have families are advised to include spouses, children, and other family members in at least some of their social activities.

The social sector is all about fun, but that doesn't mean it can't be as stressful as the other sectors of your life. As in the other sectors, if you feel social stress, it is a clue you are not following Nature's mandates. Minimize the chance for stress in the social sector by choosing social contacts whose interests are similar to yours and who are mature adults. If you have had the tendency in the past to choose friends who like drama and conflict, examine your motives and consider the predictable consequences. Is the stress involved in having an unstable, undependable friend really worth the thrill? The purpose of social activity is to connect with others and blow off steam. If you ever regret your behavior in a social situation or with a particular group of people, perhaps that situation or group is not the right one for you. Keep searching for social contacts and circumstances that make you feel good, but not at your own or anyone else's expense.

Nature holds us all accountable for our actions. The early tone we set in the social sector can benefit us or hinder us for the remainder of our lives. Handled properly, the social sector can be an enormous asset to building powerful social networks, which will not only help the individual but also the rest of the world.

The three divisions of the mind (instinctual, intellectual, and emotional) and the five sectors of life (physical, professional, personal, financial, and social) play an important role in defining our identity, determining our behavior, and influencing the direction of our lives. Nature has assigned certain responsibilities to each of these categories, and by meeting these obligations, we can make our journey through this life much smoother than it would otherwise be. Each of us must balance the three aspects of our minds and fine-tune the sectors of our lives according to our individual strengths and weaknesses. In general, some sectors of life take more work than others. For example, the professional and financial sectors need more attention than the social sector. Domestic partnership occurs in the personal sector but affects the social and financial sectors and therefore requires a delicate balance. When a sector is neglected, poorly managed, or disabled by an event or our own innate defects—for example, cancer or ADHD (physical sector), the death of a child (personal sector), unemployment (professional sector), foreclosure of your home (financial sector), or cyber bullying (social sector)—the resulting imbalance has a negative impact on the other sectors and quality of life, thus causing widespread stress. It is critical to our success and stability to safeguard the integrity of all the sectors to the best of our abilities. Our instincts, intellect, and emotions can help us understand Nature's mandates for each sector, leading toward harmony among the sectors and a stress-free life.

Once you have begun the process of getting to know yourself and balancing the various aspects that make up your identity, you are ready to establish where and how you fit into this world. This step is very important, because the world is the stage where your performance matters most to you and to others. Therefore, it is imperative you see the world as it exists, which will optimize your chances to lead a secure, successful, and stress-free life. The more you know about the world, the easier it is to find your place in it and to support yourself as well as the people who count on you.

This world is not a playground, as many would have us believe. Instead, it is a battleground, and the rules of engagement are constantly changing. We inhabit a dynamic planet equipped with plentiful natural resources and millions of plant, animal, and virus species ranging from single-cell amoebas to complex human beings. By virtue of our powerful minds and versatile bodies, humans have climbed to the top of the food chain and dominated this world. Over the years, this world has become increasingly complex and increasingly focused on global interdependence.

It might comfort us to remember, however, that one factor has remained constant throughout the ages: human nature. The dynamic between an ever-changing cultural context and unchanged human behavior is one of the most striking features of our world. In the past, human beings killed and hurt each other for trivial reasons. We continue to kill and hurt each other for trivial reasons today, the only difference being that we use more accurate, sophisticated, and lethal weapons. Some things don't change, and in the twenty-first century, humans continue to be as selfish, jealous, ambitious, belligerent, prejudiced, and shortsighted as ever. To be successful in such a world, we must be as alert, agile, affable, and assertive as our ancestors were. These attributes lead to success even in the most fiercely competitive environment.

Even as we resist internal change, humans have actively and enthusiastically effected change in the world. The climate has changed. Old species have disappeared. We have changed our lifestyles dramatically through the expansion of science and technology—fast cars, space shuttles, computers, cell phones, and fast food are part of everyday life in many cultures. Compared to previous eras, life in this century moves more quickly and offers more conveniences. Yet the basic struggle for survival for the majority of the world's population has remained an uphill battle. We have not solved world hunger or civil unrest. Our peace of mind has been battered by ongoing worldwide economic turmoil and a visible upsurge of unrest and violence (for example, the Arab Spring).

Change is constant. The shifts in economic, political, cultural, and ideological tides keep us guessing. For example, outsourcing to developing countries over the past decade has had a profound negative impact on the job opportunities and individual finances in countries like the United States. If the United States fails to adapt to these changes, it will lose its economic standing in the world. Similarly, if individuals in the current job market fail to adjust to the more competitive climate, they might find themselves out of work. Irrespective of the number of years you have loyally served an organization, if you don't anticipate the changes happening around you and make necessary adjustments to your skills and attitude, you risk losing your foothold. In a rapidly changing environment, what you learn today may be obsolete tomorrow.

This aspect of the world is nothing to fret over. Rather, it is an unavoidable reality of life and one to take in stride. With a matter-of-fact attitude, we can be vigilant to the changes occurring in the world around us and proactive in keeping up with those changes. There is nothing wrong with continuing to learn; in fact, it is preferable in all areas. In the medical field, for example, the introduction of fiber optics, miniature cameras, powerful microscopes, and lasers, to name a few recent technologies, has changed the dynamics of diagnosing and treating many illnesses. Whereas a surgeon in the past treated gastrointestinal ailments such as perforated gastric ulcers or colon cancers through major surgery, the advent of endoscopies and powerful cancer drugs has eliminated the need for surgical intervention in many such cases. Certainly this is good news for the patient, but the surgeon must be retrained in more current, less-invasive procedures using the latest technology if he or she intends to thrive as a surgeon.

Where do you fit in this complex world? Among all the species on Earth, we face the greatest challenge, because Nature has given us the gift of complex consciousness. Finding your place in this world depends on how well you understand yourself and interact with your fellow human beings. This task has to be accomplished alone, even if you are fortunate enough to have close family and friends. Your mission in at its root is a solitary one, yet, in order to survive you must persuade other people to work in your favor without compromising the laws of Nature.

A CASE IN POINT: My colleague loved to go fishing in his spare time. He would charter a boat with his friends and spend weekends catching fish. Over the years, he became an expert fisherman. He knew the right times and locations to catch big fish like bass, flounder, and cod. He dreamed of one day owning a comfortable boat where he could spend weekends and holidays with his family and friends. Unfortunately, he had to support a big family and was always short on cash. But he did not give up on his dream. He found out that local restaurant owners were willing to pay good money for fresh catch. He made a deal with a few of them to deliver fish, and with the money they paid him, he was able to save a down payment for his boat. The money he continued to make selling his catch allowed him to make payments on his boat. In this way, he realized his dream. In this world we can negotiate our way toward what we want using what Nature has given us: imagination, ingenuity, and willingness to work hard.

If we expect others to cooperate with us as we strive to reach our goals, we must both establish our own credibility and evaluate the credibility of those with whom we are working. Being credible means expressing beliefs, goals, and intentions in a straightforward and sincere manner. While we can establish our own credibility by behaving honorably whenever possible, we cannot, unfortunately, always trust others to do the same. We can never be sure of someone else's true intentions, because we cannot read each other's minds. The information we receive from another person is only as credible as the source—most information should be taken with a grain of salt. People will usually tell us what they want us to hear rather than the truth, which is what we need to hear. Some people are masters at concealing their intentions and feelings. Trust is therefore a rare and precious commodity. If you can trust only one other individual without any reservations, consider yourself lucky. You must rely on yourself to judge whom to believe, whom to trust, and what to realistically expect from a person, based on his or her character, reputation, and past behavior. When we expect the most from ourselves and little from the world and the other people in it, we are rarely disappointed but often pleasantly surprised.

The world will never bend over backward to accommodate our needs, and to expect it to do so is an exercise in futility. We must prepare ourselves for a tough fight in order to succeed. To paraphrase Pulitzer Prize–winning journalist George Will, it's not the size of the dog in the fight that counts, it's the size of the fight in the dog. It's best to bring a certain attitude to the fight: We can build strong, comfortable, binding relationships with this world by responding to life's challenges with patience, tolerance, flexibility, perseverance, and realistic expectations. We must never expect the world to concern itself with our goals, our agendas, or our missions. The sooner we accept this reality, the easier it will be to work toward our goals.

This world will cooperate with you fully only if your task is beneficial to the world. If you have a project and need the world's help to complete it, take the time to prepare a comprehensive presentation to convince the powers that be that it is in their best interest to cooperate with you. Preparing such a presentation will also help you to see clearly the strengths and weaknesses of your project. If your presentation is successful, not only will the necessary participants cooperate with you, the world might deliver success to you on your terms. Your window of opportunity, however, will exist only for a limited time. If you intend to convince the world that it needs you as much as you need it, consider that the human attention span is shorter than ever. Expect to hold your audience's attention for no longer than five minutes. Within that time frame, create a presentation that is informative, interesting, and to the point.

Understanding and balancing your mind and the various sectors of your life are classified as internal affairs. Tasks requiring the world's participation and cooperation are external affairs. If you decide to open a restaurant, for example, irrespective of your internals—your talents, interests, and desires—you need the external cooperation of the world to make your business a successful venture. If you actually get your restaurant off the ground and people enjoy the cuisine and ambiance, you will stay in business. When you work on external affairs, you will have only partial control over what happens. You can study the demographic of the area in which your restaurant will be located, and after opening, you can do your homework to learn the tastes and eating habits of your customers and make the appropriate adjustments to your menu. You can do your best and hope to succeed in your endeavor. But you must also accept, without fear or despair, that many factors influencing your business are out of your control. For instance, in an economic downturn, people may not have the money to eat out. As in any other situation, your job is to control what you can control and not worry about the rest.

As we search for our place in the world, it is important to ask, *How might I advance my own cause while also serving others?* No one can answer this question but you. Regardless of how others behave, we should aspire to think beyond our own survival and consider how we might utilize our talents to make this world a better place. We are all human beings trying to get by. Some of us are born into comfort and plenty, while others are born into hardship. Those are the cold facts. But we all occupy the same planet and all depend upon its vast resources to survive. We are all connected by this need, and each of us is obligated to safeguard the world's resources and help those who are less fortunate. The survival of our species depends upon altruism, our impulse to help others in need. Not to mention that it feels good! Find ways to affect others in a positive way, and you will find a wonderful smile on your face. That sense of satisfaction is the key to experiencing unadulterated peace of mind, perhaps the most valuable commodity one can possess. Opening ourselves to the truth of our place in this world can be challenging and at times scary. But if you examine the opportunities around you with courage, clarity, and confidence, you will ace the task of using the wits and talents Nature gave you to their best effect. As you can see, finding your place in the world can be enormously invigorating and exciting.

# Part II

# Special Topics in Stress

*Six*

---

# Stress in Children

*by Preetham Grandhi*

Children are people too, and therefore, they are prone to stress. Unlike adults, however, children do not have the tools or knowledge to identify the sources of their stress or to express how the stress is affecting them or even how to tackle the problem properly. Their abilities to cope with stress independently vary with their developmental ages. They often do not know how to seek help when faced with a stressful situation. Considering these vulnerabilities, it is incumbent upon a child's parents or caregivers to recognize the signs of stress in the child. To this end, we must address the following questions:

- What are the origins of childhood stress?
- What role do parents play in creating and conquering childhood stress?
- What does stress in children look like?
- How do children express stress?
- Is childhood stress different from adult stress?
- Is there an effective way to give every child a stress-free childhood?

## PARENTING AND THE ORIGINS OF STRESS

The origins of childhood stress reach back to the time before birth. We would like to think that in utero we are protected from the harsh

111

world outside. But even a fetus has to endure physical and environmental stressors. For example, chemical compounds such as prescription and nonprescription drugs, cigarette smoke, alcohol, and high levels of stress in the mother have a negative effect on fetal development and can even result in abortion or premature birth. Not only do environmental stressors have immediate consequences for the fetus, but the signs of stress can also be apparent after birth in the physical and mental development of the child. Studies have shown links between fetal stress and learning disabilities, physical handicaps, and mental retardation.[1]

For the best results after birth, an expectant mother can take every reasonable precaution to protect the fetus from environmental stressors. The role of the father during pregnancy is as important as the role of the mother. From Nature's point of view, it is the duty of the father to help create a safe and stress-free environment for the mother and the child she is carrying. In addition, the father must pay special attention to the needs of the expectant mother. Single expectant mothers have the double responsibility of carrying the fetus and creating a safe and stress-free environment for themselves, perhaps with the help of a support network of family members and friends.

To understand the role of parenting from Nature's point of view we need only look at how parenting happens in the rest of the natural world. My favorite example comes from the award-winning documentary *The March of the Penguins*.[2] The movie illustrates clearly that in order to have a viable penguin chick, both parents have to endure numerous hardships with little room for failure. From the conception of the egg by the mother to the passing of the egg to the father for hatching, the process is a meticulous and delicate one, with each step defined by Nature. In such a harsh and unforgiving environment, even the smallest mistake or deviation from Nature's plan means losing the offspring.

From Nature's point of view, the process of becoming parents is no different for humans. Only when we follow Nature's plan will we produce offspring able to survive and reach its full potential. As we've seen, humans have an advantage over other animal species: consciousness, as defined by the instinctual mind, the intellectual mind, and the emotional mind. Nature has given us the gift of complex thought, and along with it comes the freedom to decide our own actions and the responsibility to respect the laws of Nature.

The concept of parenthood has changed dramatically during the past two generations. Today, 25 percent of American children are being raised in single-parent households, and many gay couples are adopting children or using in vitro fertilization or artificial insemination to become parents.[3] Regardless of how a person becomes a parent, Nature expects that parent to accept the responsibility of protecting his or her child and raising that child into a strong adult.

One disturbing trend in contemporary parenting is that the responsibilities associated with a child's daily life are being delegated. Just as corporations are outsourcing certain work tasks, parents are now outsourcing their parental responsibilities. Various circumstances drive such an arrangement, including single parenting, dual-income households, irresponsible parenting, and parentless or "problem" children placed in the care of other systems, such as foster care. Whenever parental duties are outsourced, there is a negative impact on the developing child, and when nearly all parental duties are outsourced, the negative impact on not only the child but on the family unit can be dire. For instance, a child who has been raised predominantly by a nanny will bond with the nanny, not with the parents, and will soon come to see the nanny as the parental figure. The nanny will have a profound impact on the child's attitudes, outlook, and spirits. If the parent then tries to correct the child's behaviors, the child will resent the parent because of the conflict of ideology.

Children are born dependent on adults. Consequently adult choices, behaviors, and actions will have an impact on children. Adults, for their part, often seem unaware that it is an awesome responsibility to bring a child into this world. While it isn't possible to be completely prepared for parenthood, you can make a good start by being in tune with Nature's principles and carefully considering when to become a parent, preferably when you are physically, mentally, and financially able to provide for a child. At the very least, prospective parents should be able to give their children unconditional love and a feeling of security. And even when parents are prepared to give their children these things, they must understand that much of parenting is learned in real time.

The day our son was born, I was struck for the first time by an overwhelming sense that I was now a parent. Not even the previous night did I have such a feeling. Of course, we knew we were going to be parents throughout the course of the pregnancy, but this was different. As it turned out, knowing I would become a parent and becoming one were two different things. That night, I went home from the hospital where my beloved wife and newborn were bonding in harmony, but I couldn't sleep. I was having an anxiety attack. It was a joyous time, and I chided myself for not cherishing every moment of it, but I only felt the joy in fleeting glimpses.

Ten years later, I realize that I was panicking because I had become a parent, but I had no idea what that meant in practical terms. The baby had not come with a manual to tell me how to conduct my life from that point on. I thought being a child and adolescent psychiatrist and having given many patients advice on parenting would prepare me for parenthood. But in reality it was not so. Like any other parent, I would have to feel my way through it, figuring out how my wife and I could raise our child to be a happy, productive, and stress-free individual within the framework of his strengths and weaknesses.

Irrespective of their geographic location or cultural backgrounds, every parent will have to face the same challenges in raising children to become productive individuals. Whether a child is born into a family or adopted, the parents cannot predict or prepare for who that child will be. But if parents have a strong foundation built by following Nature's mandates, they will be prepared for the challenges of parenthood.

Once children enter this world, they look for a feeling of safety and security. If they do not develop a secure trusting relationship with adults by the age of two or three, they are at risk of becoming poorly functioning youths and dysfunctional adults. As with adults, children who feel any threat to their security experience stress. The loss of security is the number one source of childhood stress. Children who are feeling insecure usually withdraw from others and isolate themselves in an attempt to keep themselves safe. They might be unable to focus on everyday tasks and might experience bed-wetting and nightmares and develop poor eating habits.

A CASE IN POINT: A few years ago, I evaluated an intelligent twelve-year-old-boy named Jimmy for behavioral problems at school. He had difficulty doing his homework, but he loved playing video games, participating in extracurricular activities, and doing volunteer work. Jimmy had been adopted by his parents from Colombia when he was two. He had been born to a teenage mother who was unable to care for him and had put him up for adoption.

Jimmy had been a fussy child ever since his American parents had adopted him. By the time he was five, Jimmy knew he had been adopted. Once he learned the truth about his origins, he started to emotionally distance himself from his adoptive parents and from then on was unable to have a trusting relationship with them. This condition, called adoptive child complex, prevented Jimmy from trusting others as well as his parents. He didn't feel safe taking anyone into his confidence. In essence he isolated himself from the world in an attempt to feel safe.

His parents had a troubled marriage, which only added to the family dysfunction. Over the years, a pattern of distrust and hatred developed between the parents. Jimmy began to grow increasingly oppositional, for example choosing not to do his schoolwork as a way to express his displeasure and rebel against the stressful situation at home. By the time he was eleven, he risked failing out of even a modified educational track. He was intellectually capable of doing his schoolwork, as evidenced by psychological testing, but he lacked an interest in the work. He also harbored a lot of anger and rage. Watching him, one might have thought that he was depressed, but that was not the case.

Because Jimmy's problems were intertwined with his family's problems, I decided to work with him and his parents as a family unit. We set up a motivational plan to help him do his schoolwork, both in class and at home. However, my efforts failed to motivate him. In the follow-up family therapy sessions, it became clear that Jimmy had no respect for his parents because they were not his biological parents. Additionally, their marital problems created a stressful home environment for the entire family, and Jimmy didn't trust them to keep him safe. They had no chance of getting him to do homework under these circumstances. Even buying him gifts with no strings attached had no effect on his level of respect and trust. I realized that until he respected and trusted his parents, he would not change his ways.

By the time Jimmy's parents sought therapy for him, Jimmy was a tween, and it was too late for him to develop the attachments to his parents that would have led to a sense of security and family harmony. Unfortunately for his adoptive parents, Jimmy could not detach emotionally from an idealized biological mother, from whom he felt unfairly separated. His parents resented Jimmy for his feelings, causing even more strain in the family dynamics. Many aspects of Jimmy's life felt threatening to him, and the stress he felt almost constantly made him increasingly bitter and angry.

Eventually, in private sessions with Jimmy, I was able to persuade him to take me into his confidence. During our conversations, I convinced him to cut his adoptive parents some slack. Under my guidance he became less angry at the situation and began to work with them. From Jimmy's perspective, his life had been filled with threats to his security since he was a small child. His mind had created an internal threat by fixating on his separation from his biological mother, and he created the story in his mind that only if he was reunited with her would he be safe. This in turn produced a constant feeling of insecurity. His parents added to that feeling of insecurity by creating external threats to Jimmy's peace of mind in the form of the discord between them and their resentment toward Jimmy himself. Finally, the expectations about school added another layer of external threats to Jimmy's peace of mind. What Jimmy didn't realize was that his response to the stress in his life was hurting him the most. It was in his best interest to learn how to conquer his stress rather than react blindly to it.

The struggle for biological identity among adopted children can be a source of stress. Whether prospective parents are thinking about adoption or has already adopted, Jimmy's case raises three important questions:

- Should adopted parents keep the child's biological heritage or origin from the adopted child? What would be the pros and cons of doing so?
- When and how should the parents disclose the adoption?
- How does the parent deal with the aftermath of such a disclosure?

The disclosure of adoption is a complex and sensitive issue for both adoptive parent and child. There is no standard method to make this disclosure, and it is difficult to predict the reaction of the adopted child once they learn about their adoption. The outcome depends on the age of the child when adopted, the circumstances of the adoption, and the parent-child match.

I believe a child must be told of the adoption. A parent who truly loves and cares for the child must be truthful. There is no effective set age to tell a child about the adoption, especially for children who were adopted as infants or preverbal toddlers. It is a process that occurs over time and can begin as early as three years of age. Depending on the age and the cognitive abilities of the child, the information must be tailored to their developmental level and given over a period of time.

Adoption is further complicated if the ethnicity of the child does not match that of the parents or the child has been adopted by a gay or lesbian couple. Typically, children begin to have questions and feelings about their biological identities and biological families because they notice the obvious differences. Such special circumstances warrant an earlier disclosure. Initially there may be some setbacks, especially if the child is a preschooler or adolescent when told. In time, parental love and support will heal the child's wounds and help them move on. This must be done in a gentle and loving way, thus reflecting the continued security from the adoptive parents.

It is often easier to gain emotional closure when the adoption is due to parental death. Any other kind of adoption leaves room for the feeling of having been rejected by the biological parents, leading to an "Adoption Complex" and a sense of not belonging that can impede upon the parent-child relationship. Not disclosing such information can lead to guilt and stress in the adoptive parent. If the child finds out the truth from another source, then the child will not forgive the adoptive parents, leading to dissolution of trust. In this way both parent and child will experience chronic ongoing stress.

No matter when and how the adoption is disclosed, it is expected that there will be emotional reactions to the information. This does not necessarily reflect on who the parent is or their parenting capabilities but rather a normal reaction to the news of adoption. The parent has to listen, be patient with, and understand these expected emotions such as anger and sadness, be prepared to guide and answer any questions that arise, and, most important, always be there for the child.

As we saw with Jimmy's case, parental infighting, parental addictions, and parental separation have a serious negative impact on the psyche of a child and make daily life for that child inordinately stressful. A disruptive family environment fosters confusion and insecurity, which can lead to learning disabilities, poor social skills, lack of interest, lack of focus, and inability to engage in and complete a task. Ultimately, a child may withdraw from his immediate surroundings to escape the confusion of the home environment. To make matters worse for the child, such behavioral problems are often incorrectly labeled as depression or ADHD and treated with medications, the effects of which lead to more mental and physical problems. Unfortunately, children of dysfunctional homes suffer serious consequences through no fault of their own and pay a heavy price for the rest of their lives. Make no mistake, parents' emotional and behavioral problems certainly visit themselves on their children. The younger the child, the greater the impact.

A few lucky children survive disruptive homes unscathed, but they are in the minority. Most children grow to be adults with adjustment problems. For these children and the adults they become, learning to abide by Nature's mandates, whether through philosophy or psychotherapy, can address these adjustment problems and lead to stress-free living. However, unlike adult behavioral difficulties such as obesity or addiction, some children's behavioral problems are not the result of their environment but of genetic or innate deficits. Still other children have a combination of innate and behavioral deficits. It is important for the sake of a fulfilling family life that we understand these deficits and how Nature's mandates can help overcome them.

## HARDWARE AND SOFTWARE: THE BRAIN AND THE MIND

There is some discussion in scientific circles regarding whether the brain or the mind controls human behavior. Neuroscientists and psychopharmacologists believe the brain is in charge. Cognitive behavior therapists and psychotherapists credit the mind for behavior. Based on my study and experience, I think that behavioral issues stem from deficits either in the brain or in the mind or in a combination of the two. A computer model is useful in describing the relationship between the mind and the brain, where the physical brain acts as the hardware, and the mind, an abstract collection of thoughts and ideas, acts as the software. The brain hosts the mind, but as Pavlov proved beyond doubt, the mind has considerable influence over both the brain and behavior. For example, just the thought of eating something delicious (an idea in the mind) triggers the salivary glands (a physical process ordered by the brain). According to the strengths and weaknesses doled out by Nature, some of us are born with hardware that has capacities of the first Macintosh and some of us with capabilities like the latest iMac. Most of us fall somewhere in between. Similarly, we might be said to have Windows DOS when we're born, with our software developing over the years into something more closely resembling Windows 7. The brain serves no purpose without the mind, like a computer with no software. Conversely, the software cannot exist if there is no hardware to support it. Hence the mind and brain are codependent and of no value independent of one another.

Stress is a problem of the mind and not of the brain. A hardware (brain) defect might exist, but it is the mind that suffers from the conflicts created by that internal source of stress. Numerous childhood disorders can become a source of stress, such as ADHD, autism, depression, anxiety disorders, childhood bipolar disorder, and childhood schizophrenia. Many of these disorders have genetic and neurobiological expressions that result in faulty hardware, which in turn leads to mind functions that don't conform to societal norms, thereby causing conflict and stress for children and parents.

Hardware problems, such as autism, are innate, whereas software issues, such as some mood disorders like depression, are acquired. These differences make it imperative that we identify the roots of a childhood behavioral problem and treat it accordingly. Software problems, for example, need not be treated with medication. Many parents despair to learn that no device or drug can treat autism, since nothing can correct the traits in the brain that cause this ailment. Only intense personal attention and psychotherapy can make an appreciable improvement in an autistic child's behavior. It is a tragic fact that the stress involved in managing autistic children has broken up many families. When both parents of an autistic child share the responsibility and support each other, however, the child can only benefit.

Similarly, evidence suggests that clinical depression is due to a chemical imbalance or defect in the hardware, or the brain itself, and should be treated with appropriate medication, supported by psychotherapy. However, sensitive children may react to disappointment and disenchantment with behavior resembling depression, which is frequently diagnosed as clinical depression and treated with medication to no avail. In such cases, it becomes apparent that the problem is a matter of the mind and should be treated instead through philosophical psychotherapy if the child is old enough and mature enough to benefit from it.

Attention deficit hyperactivity disorder (ADHD) can be seen as a neurodevelopmental variation of normal development—a hardware difference, if not necessarily an abnormality. The neuronal pathways in certain children may develop at a different pace when compared to the majority of children. This difference in the developmental trajectory can cause the child with ADHD to stick out like a sore thumb among a group of other children whose developmental trajectories look similar. This in turn can isolate the ADHD child from peers and cause psychological stress that further worsens the condition.

Generally, ADHD is treated with medications, such as Adderall and Ritalin, because the condition is considered to originate in the hardware, or brain. However, many children have been misdiagnosed with ADHD, and thus when they are treated with such medications, the results are disappointing. I have come to believe that many of these behavioral conditions are mainly software problems and have little to do with hardware. In these cases where hardware problems have been ruled out, psychotherapy based on the laws of Nature is an appropriate approach and yields gratifying results. However, many individuals with ADHD are too young to understand and adapt sound philosophical ideas. They may therefore need some form of pharmacological therapy until they are mature enough to make the best use of psychotherapy.

A CASE IN POINT: Alex was a six-year-old boy with a loving

personality and lots of energy, but with the attention of a flea. He loved getting involved in any activity, but he had difficulty completing any of them. In kindergarten his hyperactive behaviors were seen as a variant of other normal children's behaviors. He would not finish any task fully and would get into trouble for not staying on task and for interrupting other students in class. By the end of kindergarten, he was experiencing a lot of stress. The threat to his peace of mind was both internal—his inability to stay on task—and external—his constant conflicts with his teachers, who were always correcting his behavior. He could not understand why everything that went wrong seemed to be his fault. As a result, he began to develop a low self-esteem and an overwhelming sense of failure.

It was clear to me from the moment he stepped into my office that Alex had ADHD. I suggested appropriate medications for his condition. However, his mother, a psychologist, was skeptical about using such powerful medications for her son at such a young age. When I convinced her that properly diagnosed ADHD is truly a neurobiological (hardware) issue that should be treated with medications, she decided to try the medications.

Alex himself was afraid of swallowing pills. After some coaxing from his mother, he began taking Concerta, a long-acting formulation of Ritalin used to treat ADHD. A few days later, there was an appreciable difference in his performance at school. Once Alex was able to focus on the task at hand, he was also able to blend in with the other children in his class. He was no longer singled out by his teachers. His stress disappeared, and as it did, his self-confidence rose. He became a star pupil. As I told Alex's mother, it is possible that when Alex is older, he may not need medication. As an adult, he will have the opportunity to develop coping skills to manage the deficit that Nature had imposed on him. There are many children like Alex with underlying biological psychiatric disorders. These children can be susceptible to stress that can in turn lead to depression or anxiety disorders. Luckily, such problems can be managed, even at a young age.

I firmly believe that a brain function rather than a mind function was at the root of Alex's stress response. As we've determined, stress itself is a problem of the mind rather than the brain, a problem with software rather than hardware. But a child's expression of stress can be similar to the symptoms of a more profound psychiatric disorder, such as clinical depression. That is why it is of the utmost importance for the adults in a child's life to determine the root cause of the child's stress. In this day and age, busy parents are often unwilling to take the time to deal appropriately with their children's stress. Many of them opt for quick fixes through psychotropic medications. Unfortunately, medications given inappropriately usually make matters worse.

## A CHILD'S RESPONSE TO STRESS

A more benign source of stress in children is the word *no*, which creates instant conflict between the child and the speaker. For example, let's say a parent and a child visit a store on an errand. The child sees a toy that she wants, but the parent responds to the request by saying, "No." At this point, the emotional aspect of the child's mind despairs with a primal intensity to be expected in a child. The child begins to cry wildly in what adults call a "tantrum." The event is stressful for both the child and the parent, not to mention the onlookers.

When parents view events like this one from the child's point of view, they might understand that everyone would be better off if, in a similar situation, they would engage the child's intellect and instincts to offset the inevitable emotional response. Instead of responding with the word "no," which often elicits a psychological knee-jerk reaction, a parent might deliver the same message less directly, giving the child time to consider what the words mean. For example, a parent might say, "We're not here to buy toys today. We need (you fill in the blank— for example, groceries)." This exchange also offers a brief lesson in the financial sector of life, namely wants versus needs. A parent might also help the child identify her emotional response by saying something like, "I'm sorry you're disappointed."

Such conflicts between parents and children will be the potential source of stress throughout the growing years and beyond. The ability to manage this conflict becomes better once the child is more able to lead with the intellect rather than the emotions. Until then, parents have to have a lot of patience and well-defined boundaries. Children who are taught to follow Nature's mandates will begin to view conflicts merely as problems to solve rather than sources of stress.

The best gift a parent can give to a child is to model how to conquer stress. Conversely, stressed-out parents pass both the stress itself and the faulty coping mechanisms down to their children. The younger the child, the harder the impact. Young children have little control over their own lives and are dependent on adults for survival, which includes love and security. It is every parent's responsibility to shield their children from their own stress while at the same time teaching children how to cope with the internal and external threats to their peace of mind.

A CASE IN POINT: Mrs. Smith came to see me with her thirteen-year-old daughter, Carrie, because Carrie refused to go to school. Many children between the ages of five and eight years old develop separation anxiety as an expression of the insecurity they're feeling, and many of them refuse to go to school. However, it was unusual to see a case of separation anxiety leading to school refusal at Carrie's age.

During my initial interview with Mrs. Smith, I learned that Carrie had suddenly decided that she did not want to go to school. She started getting up late and would purposely miss the school bus. When her mother tried to take her to school, she would have violent tantrums, and even getting her to the car was a nightmare. The strange part was that Carrie had always been an A student and had never had any kind of behavioral problems previously.

Carrie was an only child. She had been close to her father, who had passed away when she was ten years old. With the help of her mother, Carrie had worked through the loss of her father, and since then, she had done well both at home and at school. Then she suddenly became confrontational with her mother and adamantly refused to go to school. She told her mother that she was having anxiety attacks.

During my private interview with Carrie, I asked her if something at school was causing her anxiety. But the more I asked her about her anxiety, the more defensive she became. Finally she refused to answer any more of my questions, and when I asked her why, she said, "Because they're silly."

"But how can I help you if I don't know what is bothering you?" I asked.

"You can't help me," she said, her eyes starting to well with tears.

"Why not?" I asked softly.

"Because my mother has a boyfriend, and you can't make him disappear," she replied.

She told me that until recently her mother had not dated anyone since Carrie's father had died. It was immediately clear to me that Carrie was reacting to this new person her mother had introduced into their lives. Her anxiety had nothing to do with school. Once I suggested this idea, Carrie opened up. She admitted that she was scared and stressed that she would lose her mother to this new man.

I realized then that I had to first work with Mrs. Smith, not Carrie. When I talked with Mrs. Smith, I helped her understand the role of a single parent, which means taking on the responsibilities of two parents that Nature intended. Unfortunately, Nature does not relax its rules to accommodate us, and Mrs. Smith would have to make some sacrifices for Carrie's sake. I explained that Carrie was still emotionally fragile because of the loss of her father. Carrie interpreted her mother's dating as an imminent threat: she was afraid of losing her only remaining parent and being left alone. The situation had caused Carrie to panic, and she had refused to go to school as part of her irrational plan to monitor her mother all the time.

While it was understandable that Mrs. Smith would seek companionship after the death of her husband, I told her that she would have to put her relationship with her boyfriend on hold. Instead, I suggested she take the time to convince Carrie that she had nothing to fear and that she would continue to have her mother's undivided attention. Once Carrie felt secure and comfortable again, Mrs. Smith could bring up the topic of the new person in their life and convince her that he would be good for both of them.

Mrs. Smith followed my advice and told her new companion that he would have to wait until Carrie was ready to accept their relationship. Her mother's actions made Carrie feel safe, her symptoms abated, and she started going to school once again. Over the next few months, I worked with them, focusing on the mother-daughter relationship. I helped Carrie soothe the primal emotions she was experiencing and understand with all three aspects of her mind that her mother meeting another man didn't mean that Carrie was going to lose her or that her mother was betraying her deceased father.

Then one day Carrie said to me, "I don't need to come see you anymore."

I asked, "Why not?"

"My mother can go on a date, and I won't be scared or jealous."

That was the last time I saw them. Mrs. Smith and Carrie's situation is not uncommon. If Mrs. Smith had been insensitive to Carrie's stress and continued dating, the results would have been disastrous for both of them. But by putting Carrie's interests first, Mrs. Smith was able to conquer the stress in their lives and eventually meet her own needs as well. Nature expected Mrs. Smith's decisions to be guided by her parental instincts rather than her emotions in this situation. In the end, Mrs. Smith prevailed because she obeyed the laws of Nature.

Children primarily react to stress by either internalizing it or externalizing it. When children internalize stress, they withdraw from the world and those around them. They may seem depressed and anxious. When children externalize stress, they express conflict by acting out. Younger children might have temper tantrums and aggressive outbursts. Teenagers might rebel against their parents' rules and engage in dangerous behaviors, such as using drugs and alcohol.

A CASE IN POINT (INTERNALIZED STRESS): Dominic was a thirteen-year-old boy I had seen a few years ago. His aunt had brought him to my office because he had become increasingly withdrawn and uninterested in life. At first glance one might have thought that he had major depression, but on further exploration it became clearer that he had withdrawn as a reaction to stress.

Dominic's parents divorced when he was young. He lived with his father, who was a hard working electrician trying his best to meet all his son's needs. His aunt was involved in Dominic's care and was concerned about his performance in school because he was on the verge of failing seventh grade, even though he was intelligent and capable.

Over the course of a few weeks, I developed a relationship with Dominic. During one of our conversations, he expressed how disappointed he was that his mother had left him. But more so, he felt frustrated that his father was difficult to please because it always had to be his father's way or no way. He found his father to be narrow-minded and rigid. Besides, he had a  hard time concentrating in school and found himself distracted by the slightest noise. He complained of his forgetfulness in doing his school assignments, which caused a lot of arguments with his father. He was bitter about being different than the other kids and that nothing in life came easily to him.

It was clear that Dominic had Inattentive Attention Deficit Disorder, which is a subtype of ADHD. When I explained it to him, he was angry that he had ADHD because it made him feel like a misfit. He was jealous of his peers because they did not have to work twice as hard to get the same results. The disparity between how he envisioned his life versus the reality of his life created stress that consumed his energy and sapped his spirits. He did not know how to deal with his feelings or how to fix his situation. He became sullen and isolated and withdrew into a cocoon of self-pity.

Over the next few weeks, I helped Dominic to understand that he did not have a choice to whom he was born or what he would be born with—like talents, intellect, and so forth. I convinced him that he really had a loving father despite an inflexible personality. I explained that he had only two choices to his predicament with his father: either he could accept the way his father was and work with him or go back in time and change his parents.  At the same time, he also needed to accept what Nature had bestowed upon him in terms of his attention capacities. I told him that medications can help decrease the inattention and help him with school work, but only a positive outlook and healthy attitude would enable him to progress in life.

We both knew that going back in time was impossible. When Dominic realized that his father indeed loved him and that it was not possible for him to change his father but rather his own outlook and approach to life, he began to come out of his shell —he had reached his Turning Point. I took time to speak to his father about Dominic's feelings. I told him that it's not easy being a single parent and he's doing a wonderful job of providing for his son. He just needed to express his love and affection toward Dominic. I reminded his father that a show of affection, even if it's difficult for him, was necessary to bring Dominic emotionally closer to him and make Dominic feel secure.

Dominic began to overlook his father's quirks and was determined to be "better" than his father by being more flexible and open-minded. He accepted the fact that he would have to work harder than his peers, and with a little help of medication, creativity, and strategy his inattention could easily be overcome. This meant an end to his conflict and thus an end to his stress. By the time he ended his treatment with me, his attitude had changed and his life was back on track. By the way, with after-school tutoring he passed seventh grade.

A CASE IN POINT (EXTERNALIZED STRESS): The first time I met Mary was the day after she had been admitted to the inpatient hospital unit. She stood in front of me, half my size and a little small for a nine-year-old. Her face was dominated by her shiny big brown eyes and a big smile. She looked up into my eyes and asked me, "Can I make a phone call?"

I smiled at her and said, "Not now, because it's not phone hour. But maybe later this evening you can make your call."

Before I could continue, the deep brown skin of her face turned maroon. She whipped around and started screaming at the top of her lungs, demanding that she be allowed at that very moment to make the phone call to which she was certainly entitled. She stalked around the lobby of the unit clenching her small fist, snarling and growling under her breath. I stepped back slowly into the nurses' station and shut the bottom half of the Dutch door, hoping she would not lash out physically and hurt herself or someone else.

It was clear that my refusal had evoked a strong primitive response in Mary, during which her mind was flooded with intense anger and rage to the point that any intellectual thinking had been thrown out of the window. It was as though this was the first time Mary had heard the word "no." In reality, I knew she had heard it many times, but not with any authoritative value attached to it. Under certain circumstances, Mary knew that "no" often meant "yes," so she had never experienced its true meaning.

As I watched her through the Plexiglas surrounding the nurses' station, Mary continued to scream and shout. She banged on the window, implying that she meant business. I spoke over her loud voice, saying, "There's no need to be upset. We can talk about it when you calm down."

I could now see why she had come to the hospital. This was her first hospitalization but her tenth round with a new foster family. Every round with a foster family meant more uncertainty, which caused stress. Mary had been such a terror in each of those foster homes and had caused so much emotional upheaval that the only choice the foster parents felt they had was to get rid of her.

It took five minutes for Mary to calm down enough to have a more meaningful conversation. She came back to the Dutch door of the nurses' station and sulked.

"I want to make a phone call now," she demanded in a calmer manner.

"Do you know what the word *no* means?" I asked her.

"No," she scowled.

"That's exactly what it means. What you just said is exactly what it means."

Mary did not like what she was hearing. She stood at the door huffing and puffing. I waited again for this stage of the tantrum to subside.

"You need to be in school, you know," I continued.

"No, I don't want to go to school!" she said loudly.

"There are benefits to going to school," the nurse on the unit chimed in.

"You're the one who needs an education," Mary snapped.

"But if you don't go to school, then you won't be able to attend the Christmas party later this week," I said and left it at that.

Mary stood silently for five minutes weighing her options. She then in a polite but sad voice said, "I want to go to school now."

I looked at her and said, "That's a good choice, but you'll have to wait for a staff member to come and take you to school."

"I want to go now," Mary said, her voice rising again. "Right now!"

It was clear from our interaction that if Mary's requests were not immediately gratified, she became stressed. She externalized her stress, expressing it through violent temper tantrums.

The foster care agency working on her case told me that Mary was the oldest of five siblings born to a teenage mother. She and her siblings had been removed from their mother's care because of neglect. Mary had grown up without adult supervision, and as the oldest child, she had at a young age assumed the role of caretaker for her four younger siblings. As a parental figure, she set the rules for the household and did not have to be accountable to anyone. That is why she had never heard the word "no." To make things worse, she had fallen far behind in school because she didn't attend for weeks at a time.

Mary had never had the chance to be a child. While her emotions were raw and immature, she was forced to assume the role of an adult. While she was the security blanket for the other members of her family, she never felt secure herself. She had never received one word of appreciation or encouragement from her own mother. When she was taken from the only home she knew and placed in a foster home, she was no longer the disciplinarian and instead was being disciplined by strangers, a dynamic she deeply resented.

I realized that the key to working with her and winning her trust would be to empathize with her situation and recognize a job well done given her circumstances. Once I earned her trust, it was easy for us to discipline and train her to control her anger. The hospital environment made her feel safe and secure; a daily routine under the supervision of the staff taught her the importance of taking care of herself, which improved her self-esteem. Attending the hospital school, she learned how to cooperate with other children and began to enjoy the experience of playing and learning new things. Her experience in the hospital mellowed her emotions and allowed her to operate more from her instincts and intellect. Over the many months she spent on the unit, this corrective experience was reinforced, and she was taught how to communicate via more sophisticated verbal expression rather than immature temper tantrums. Gradually she became less belligerent and more cooperative with the staff. Once the three aspects of her mind were more balanced and she was operating from a position of security rather than insecurity, she had a chance of having a better relationship with her future foster parents.

## STRESS-INDUCED DISORDERS IN CHILDREN

Mental health professionals use *The Diagnostic and Statistical Manual of Mental Disorders* (DSM IV) to help identify and treat stress-related disorders in children, which are disorders of the mind rather than the brain. The DSM IV classifies stress disorders based on whether the stressor is associated with daily life or with a traumatic event. Many stressors are common in daily life, including the following:

- School performance
- Homework
- Peer pressure
- Conflicting parent-child expectations
- Conflicts between other family members, such as sibling rivalry or arguing between parents or caregivers
- Divorce
- Physical and mental handicaps
- Limited parental financial capacity
- Lack of attention from caregivers
- Lack of opportunity and resources

Children who respond to the stressors of daily life by developing emotional or behavioral symptoms such as restlessness, moodiness, and anxiety are given the diagnosis of adjustment disorder. Children, especially young children, need the assistance of the adults in their lives to help them overcome the negative effects stress can have on their lives. Adjustment disorder can often be resolved by parental intervention and consultation with a mental-health professional.

Unlike adults, children cannot conquer stress. Children are not intellectually or emotionally mature enough to understand the dynamics of stress and come up with strategies to vanquish it alone. Parents, caregivers, or other adults are responsible for protecting children from stress and guiding them through the daily challenges that life presents. Children who are guided in this way can overcome adjustment disorders and gradually develop the confidence they need to conquer stress. In most cases, young adults from the late teens to the early twenties should be capable of tackling stress on their own with minimal supervision from adults.

While protecting a child from stress, adults must lay the groundwork for children to take over the task. Guidelines for laying the groundwork include the following:

- *Stressed-out parents breed stressed-out children.* Parents must first conquer stress and provide a peaceful, secure environment for the child.

- *Children must know above all that they are loved and safe.* Children who feel secure in these ways will see many stressors as surmountable.
- *Adults should resolve their differences privately rather than in front of children.* Arguing between adults makes children sad.
- *Children depend on parents for guidance and security, not friendship.* Adults who act like their children's friends rather than parents can cause their children to feel insecure.
- *Teach your children tolerance for different religions, economic classes, ethnicities, and cultures.* This will help them feel comfortable rather than stressed among diverse groups of people.
- *Teach your children to express their ideas in a respectful, assertive manner.*
- *Teach your children from an early age the basic lessons of Nature that apply to the five sectors of life*, including to take care of their bodies, to pursue their natural interests, to develop relationships with people they trust, to tell the difference between needs and wants, and to enjoy the company of others.
- *Make sure your children are physically active from the time they are born.* Encourage them to participate in sports or other physical activities to keep their bodies strong, prevent future chronic health problems, provide an outlet for relaxation and tension release, and teach them about discipline and sportsmanship.
- *Don't overschedule your children beyond their capacities* (or yours), since it will only create stress. An overwhelmed child is unable to learn.
- *Help children break down tasks into simple components.* This will prevent them from being overwhelmed, help them to understand the task better and feel encouraged to complete the task.
- *Set aside time every day to have a meaningful conversation*

*with your children.* Actively listen to them when they talk, because it will give you insight into their world. Children whose parents listen to and empathize with them find talking with their parents comforting and invigorating. Such children will also be receptive to parental advice. Share age-appropriate life experiences with them (for example, how you solved a certain problem when you were their age) as bedtime stories.

- *Encourage children to watch documentaries about nature, the animal kingdom, and ecology.* From such programs, they will learn that the world is a challenging and often brutal place but that Nature has given us all the skills we need to survive and coexist with other life forms. They will also learn the importance of natural resources and ecological stewardship.

While the stress created by daily life can be addressed relatively easily through parenting techniques and modeling, some children experience stressors that are serious or even life threatening, among them the following:

- Domestic violence, including physical and sexual abuse
- Community and school violence, including witnessing a crime, being the victim of a crime, or perpetrating a crime
- Invasive medical procedures
- Natural disasters
- Refugee and war zone trauma, including geographical displacement and combat violence
- Terrorism
- The death of a parent, caregiver, or another person the child associates with a feeling of security

The stress that children experience as the result of a traumatic event is very different from the stress involved with the day-to-day hardships. Children who develop behavioral symptoms associated with trauma are diagnosed with either acute stress disorder or post-traumatic stress disorder (PTSD). Children with acute stress disorder appear to be in a state of shock after being exposed to life-threatening events. They feel fearful, helpless, or horrified. They might also display dissociative symptoms, such as psychological numbing, reduced awareness of their surroundings, derealization, depersonalization, and amnesia. They remember and even reexperience the trauma through recurrent images, thoughts, dreams, flashbacks, illusions, and physical sensations. Children with acute stress disorder avoid any stimuli that trigger their recollections of the trauma. They often display a heightened arousal or anxiety in the form of irritability, insomnia, hypervigilance, increased startle response, and restlessness.

If the symptoms of acute stress disorder continue for over a month, then the diagnosis is changed to post-traumatic stress disorder. Over 50 percent of children initially diagnosed with acute stress disorder develop PTSD. The expression of PTSD in children depends on the age of the child. Invariably the child displays severe distress and dysfunction. The trauma can induce neurobiological changes that further complicate the disorder. The treatment of choice is trauma-focused cognitive behavioral therapy (tf-cbt) with a skilled therapist. No medication has been proven effective in directly treating PTSD, although medications are used to treat the associated symptoms, such as depression, anxiety, and nightmares.

I have used the Turning Point Program successfully in treating children with stress and related disorders without the assistance of the Turning Point Treatments. The earliest age that the Turning Point Treatment can be used is sixteen, and its use depends on the maturity of the patient and the consent of the parent or guardian.

## PREVENTING STRESS

There is nothing more effective in the battle to conquer stress than to teach children to be immune to it in the first place. When children learn to live according to Nature's mandates, they build a fundamental base from which to fight against stress, meaning they don't have to address each individual stressor that comes along, a method that can be mentally draining and spiritually depleting.

The adults in children's lives can help them build their base by helping them

- Understand themselves, including how the mind operates and how to identify and adjust the mind-set
- Understand the world, including cultural expectations, opportunities, and interpersonal relationships
- Understand Nature's gifts and expectations

## UNDERSTANDING THE MIND-SET

In order to understand themselves, children, like adults, must become familiar with the three aspects of the mind and the dynamic between them. The interplay between the instinctual, intellectual, and emotional aspects of the mind defines the *mind-set* of every individual. Our mind-set is our basic outlook on life, which reflects our temperament and affects how we behave and even what we believe. We aren't born with a mind-set; rather it develops over time as a result of the interplay between the three aspects of the mind.

When we are born, we operate according to the cues of our instinctual mind. We cry when we're hungry or uncomfortable and stop when we're satiated or comfortable again. In general we follow Nature's inbuilt mechanisms for survival. Primitive emotions such as fear and pleasure also come into play during infancy. As we grow and begin to interact with the world, we begin to incorporate more complex emotions and habits into our repertoire. By the time we reach the age of two, our emotional and intellectual divisions are more developed and complex. This is the "Terrible Twos," a period defined by the struggle between the emerging intellect and the more powerful advanced emotions. It is only after the intellect develops further and language skills appear that we are able to use the intellect in cooperation with the emotions. The ability to soothe our primitive emotions exists at birth but is manifested in physical self-soothing methods, such as the sucking reflex.

By the age of four or five, we have acquired multiple layers of mental development such as language skills, fine motor skills, gross motor skills, listening comprehension, and verbal expression. It is at about this time that the emotional aspect of the mind develops what we commonly refer to as the "temperament," the inclination of our personality to be cheerful or short-tempered or impulsive or curious or anxious or serious. Our temperaments change little over the course of our lives. These aspects of mental development along with our temperament make up the components of our basic individual mind-set.

Our mind-set is a major part of our developing personality and identity. Sometimes a significant experience can change the mind-set to function differently, whether for better or worse. As in the development of computer software, the nascent mind-set present in us at birth can be conceptualized as Version 0. When we move from infancy to toddlerhood, we acquire new layers of development, upgrading from Version 0 to Version 1. This process continues through latency and adolescence and finally into adulthood.

As we pass through adolescence, there are noticeable changes in our outlook and behavior. For example, as adolescents, many of us feel we are invincible, as in "I can drive as fast as I want, and nothing will happen to me." This mind-set leads us to take more risks, and the kinds of risks are determined by our intellectual maturity and our level of perceived invincibility.

The mind-set continues to evolve until we reach young adulthood. When we're somewhere between the ages of eighteen and twenty-four, the evolution of the mind reaches a plateau. The older we get, the harder it is to make changes to our mind-set. It is therefore important for parents to identify their child's basic mind-set in order to consciously bolster the strengths and mitigate the deficits that may hinder their child's development. Examples of basic mind-set patterns that are commonly seen in children include:

Flexible and adaptive
Hopeful and optimistic
Warm and generous
Rigid and concrete
Anxious and avoidant
Negative and pessimistic
Needy and dependent
Self-centered and entitled
Cold and aloof
Hypervigilant and distrustful

Adults can recognize their own mind-set, but children do not have the self-awareness or insight to do so. Therefore parents or caregivers should identify the mind-set they recognize in their children and guide them accordingly. For example, if your child is negative and pessimistic, then you must recognize these traits and help your child see that sometimes it is appropriate and even beneficial to be hopeful and optimistic.

The three aspects of the mind define the mind-set. At a given moment, depending on the situation, the momentary mind-set is dominated by the intellectual or the emotional mind, operating in conjunction with the instinctual mind. A child will operate from either an instinctual-intellectual mind-set or an instinctual-emotional mind-set. Most of the time, children operate from an instinctual-intellectual mind-set, occasionally shifting to an instinctual-emotional mind-set. A good example of operating in a predominately instinctual-intellectual mind-set is when a student is typing up an assignment for school. He uses his intellect to generate ideas while also using the typing skills stored in his instincts. A child doing homework must be calm and composed in order to keep information optimally flowing and learning at its peak. A child can learn only in the instinctual-intellectual mind-set.

A good example of operating in a predominately instinctual-emotional mind-set is when a teenage driver is cut off by another driver, and he gets angry. Until that moment, he has been operating from an instinctual-intellectual mind-set, thinking about where he's going while his instincts drive the car. Once he becomes angry at the other driver, however, he shifts to an instinctual-emotional mind-set, which prompts him to shout at or even chase the other driver, while disregarding the rules, regulations, and his own safety.

When adults explain the three aspects of the mind in an elementary fashion, using specific examples from life, children can begin to understand the basic dynamics at work in the mind.

A CASE IN POINT: I met with Ashley, an eight-year-old girl who was afraid to go to bed at night alone, because she was afraid that monsters were in her room.

"Do you want to be scared of monsters and lose sleep because of them forever?"

"No," she said.

No child wants to be scared; every child naturally seeks ways to feel safe.

"Ashley," I said, "let's work together to come up with a plan so that you will no longer be scared of those monsters. First tell me, have you ever really seen a monster in your room?

"No," Ashley replied.

"Since you haven't seen them in your room, it's possible they're not even there."

She agreed that it was possible.

I told her to keep a flashlight next to her bed. "If you suspect that there is a monster in your room," I said, "take your flashlight and look for it. If you don't see the monster in the closet or under your bed, then you'll know that there is no monster."

I reassured her that monsters are more afraid of us than we are of them.

"I can understand how you feel," I added, "because I was afraid of the dark too when I was little. So I used a flashlight whenever I heard a noise or suspected that something was in my room, and when I turned my flashlight on, I could see that there was nothing in my room. It turned out it was just my imagination."

She was happy to hear my explanation and said she'd follow the plan. A few weeks later I could see a remarkable change in her mind-set, which had shifted from anxious to confident. She said that she had checked her room and found no monsters there. She boasted that she was no longer afraid of monsters.

In this way, I helped Ashley see in an elementary way how to shift her instinctual-emotional mind-set to an instinctual-intellectual mind-set. She had responded to her irrational fear with rational action and in doing so negated the source of her stress.

Parents and caregivers will be able to tell when they are engaging with a child operating in an instinctual-emotional mind-set. The younger child will be having a temper tantrum, and an adolescent will be engaged in an overheated argument. It is acceptable for children to express their thoughts and feelings when they are upset, but adults must monitor the intensity and duration of the exchange in order to determine if it has crossed the threshold of meaningful dialogue. If the adult decides that the threshold has been crossed, it is imperative that he or she insist that the child regain a sense of calm before further interaction will occur.

In preadolescent children, regaining calm can be facilitated using a calming kit. A calming kit is comprised of objects used only during a crisis and might contain a stress squeeze ball, squishy toys, scented objects, small spinning tops, and small puzzles. The child can be encouraged to use one of these objects to calm down and to return to continue the dialogue when he or she feels calmer. In adolescents the same process can be encouraged using different tasks, such as writing in a journal, listening to music, or practicing deep breathing, progressive muscle relaxation, or other physical calming skills.

This process serves two purposes: First, it helps children learn how to calm themselves, which in technical terms involves shifting from an instinctual-emotional mind-set to an instinctual-intellectual mind-set. Second, the calming process allows communication between the adult and the child to resume. Trying to communicate with a child locked into an instinctive-emotional mind-set is a spiral of unproductive emotions with no end in sight. By the time we reach mature adulthood, the two mind-sets have blended into one mind-set in which the three aspects of the mind work in harmony. This usually takes place between the ages of eighteen and twenty-three.

In addition to helping children understand the aspects of the mind, it is important that parents and caregivers help children feel at ease with their physical appearance. This area is a particularly fertile source of childhood stress, especially after puberty, and can produce lifelong insecurities and resentments, expressed as low self-esteem, lack of confidence, timidity, social awkwardness, and even eating disorders, personality disorders, mood disorders, and self-destructive behavior.

Nobody is born perfect in the physical sector—or any other sector, for that matter. There are a handful of people who are gifted with natural beauty, while others have gradients of imperfection. It is essential that children understand that the body is a vessel whose purpose is to carry us through this life, and as such it should be embraced wholly, in all its beauty and imperfection.

Teach your children to accept their physical attributes and to notice that everyone has different physical strengths and weaknesses, just as they have different strengths and weaknesses in other sectors of life. Discourage your children from comparing themselves with others, and model this behavior by avoiding comparing yourself to others or your children to siblings or friends. Notice and compliment the best things about your children's physical appearance and encourage them to capitalize on their strengths. If your children's weaknesses include characteristics such as obesity, crooked teeth, or poorly fitting clothing, take an interest in tactfully helping your children take corrective measures while taking care not to make them feel self-conscious. These measures will help decrease or even eliminate the stress generated by insecurity related to self-image, increasing the likelihood that your children will be confident when interacting with others.

## RELATING TO THE WORLD

Once children have developed some degree of self-awareness and confidence, the adults in their lives should encourage them to express their thoughts clearly and without fear in any setting. Children are less anxious and more confident in their actions if they can speak their minds freely. However, freedom to express their thoughts comes with the responsibility of gauging when it is appropriate to exercise this privilege. Teach children to listen to others and to respect other points of view before expressing their own opinions, because good listeners are savvy communicators. When they and other people have conflicting goals, help them understand when to negotiate and when to compromise.

When your child is young, watch for any innate problems with speech and language. These types of problems can be an intense source of stress for children in later years but must be identified early (preferably by eighteen months) for professional interventions to be the most effective. Children with speech and language issues hinder interaction with others and affect children's self-esteem in social settings. In puberty and adolescence, children with speech problems can become victims of bullying. The resulting stress can in turn create the kind of resentment and pent-up frustration that often leads to violence.

Encourage children to present themselves with dignity and

self-respect in public places and to resolve conflicts gracefully. Discourage the use of foul language as a barrier to meaningful conversation and a sign of disrespect for oneself and others. Knowing how to handle themselves in social situations, whether in person or online, helps children avoid the stressors that accompany so many of our daily interactions.

Life is full of harsh realities, and parents are responsible for shielding their children from these stressors, at least for a little while. As children grow and develop, there are many things parents can do to teach them how to conquer stress when the time comes for them to stand on their own two feet. Parenthood isn't about trying to control the uncontrollable aspects of the world; rather, it is about ensuring that children operate from a base of security and love throughout their lives.

Parents and caregivers also have the incredible opportunity to teach children to tune in to Nature and to follow its guidelines. Children who understand Nature know how to adapt to shifting circumstances, balance the various aspects of their lives, and capitalize on their strengths. These children have little risk of developing stress-related disorders, and their freedom from stress benefits them, their families, their communities, and even the nation.

# Seven

# Post-Traumatic Stress Disorder

On May 12, 2009, America was in for a rude awakening—the shocking early morning news that five servicemen at Camp Liberty in Iraq had been shot to death by one of their fellow soldiers, John M. Russell, a forty-five-year-old sergeant.[1] Combat stress, it seemed, had turned a man formerly described as decent and levelheaded into someone who thought his problems could be solved with the worst sort of violence. Since the invasion of Iraq and Afghanistan, American soldiers have deliberately killed their comrades on six different occasions. However, this particular incident was the worst of such attacks, with five people dead and four injured.

War brings out the worst in people. Soldiers deployed to war zones witness atrocities, often on a daily basis. They can trust no one and have to watch their backs constantly to survive. Naturally, these conditions take their toll. Since the Iraq and Afghanistan wars started, Americans have been grappling with an alarming rise in mood disorders, suicides, divorce rates, and substance abuse among returning servicemen and women.[2] These problems are the work of post-traumatic stress disorder (PTSD). When a person experiences trauma, whether from being involved in a dangerous, frightening, or life-threatening event or even witnessing one, the natural human response is stress. PTSD occurs when a person continues to feel the threat of imminent danger after—many times long after—the event has ended. In cases when traumatic events result in physical injuries, PTSD lingers even after the injuries have healed. The most serious cases of PTSD, if unchecked or untreated, can drive an individual over the edge and into insanity, as seems to have been the case at Camp Liberty.

Though we hear more about PTSD when a country is at war, there are many other events that can cause lingering irrational fear, including childhood abuse; freak accidents, such as car, plane, or train wrecks, or falling from a ladder or down a hole; being physically attacked, as in a mugging or sexual assault; being defrauded out of large amounts of money; and natural disasters, such as hurricanes, earthquakes, tsunamis, and floods.

People with PTSD are anxious and agitated, even when there is no apparent reason for them to feel that way in the present environment. They are restless, and they have trouble sleeping. As a result, they often self-medicate with prescription and nonprescription drugs, such as tranquilizers, sleep aids, beta-blockers (which block the adrenaline response that keeps PTSD sufferers feeling stressed), alcohol, marijuana, or other street drugs. People with PTSD are often bitter, belligerent, moody, and short-tempered. They tend to lash out at the world and at their loved ones. Some family members misunderstand the condition and avoid people struggling with PTSD. Some sufferers become despondent and isolate themselves, even from those they love and who love them.

A CASE IN POINT: Sylvia was a fifty-one-year-old doctor's secretary. Two years before she came to see me, she had been hit by a car driven by a reckless teenage driver who ran a red light while Sylvia was crossing the street. After she was hit, she blacked out. When she regained her senses, she was lying on the street, and there was a crowd of people around her making sure that she was all right. When she tried to sit up, she experienced excruciating pain in her waist and hips. She realized she was seriously hurt, and, because she worked in a doctor's office, she imagined the worst. She was frightened that she would be physically crippled forever. Luckily for her, the accident left her only with deep bruises, muscle contusions below her waistline, and a stable pelvic fracture. The accident did not leave her with any permanent physical damage, such as spinal cord injuries.

Still, she was badly hurt, and her physical injuries took one year and a lot of medical attention to heal. Once she realized that her physical wounds had healed to her satisfaction, she decided to resume her normal activities. When she went out for her first solo walk, however, she panicked. Her heart was pounding so hard and she was breathing so fast that she ended up running back into her house. The same thing happened when she attempted to drive her car.

Sylvia thought she would be housebound forever if she did not resolve her apparent mental block. She decided to slowly ease herself back into walking and driving by doing these things with one of her family members. To her astonishment, she was unable to do either one of these things, even when the streets were empty and her husband was by her side. As soon as she started her car, her heart would race along with the engine, and her legs would become heavy. She did not even have the nerve to shift the gear from park to drive. Crossing the streets was another disaster. Whenever she tried to step into the street, she would imagine a gigantic red car coming toward her.

She went to a therapist and was diagnosed with PTSD. She attended a few group therapy sessions for people suffering from the condition. Everyone encouraged her to stay the course and told her that soon she would be free of her symptoms. At the behest of her psychiatrist, she reluctantly started to take Xanax for anxiety and Zoloft for depression. The medications helped her to sleep better and remain calm during the day, but they did not help her overcome her PTSD. One year later, she started to lose hope of ever getting better and leading a normal life again. As her hope waned, she became more anxious, depressed, and angry. She felt sorry for her family members for what she was putting them through. At times she felt that it would have been better for everyone if she had not survived the accident. She started to cry when she said that she would be better off dead than living a tormented life.

I told Sylvia that there was hope for her and that I thought she could be free of PTSD if she was ready and willing to follow certain ground rules that reflect the laws of Nature. I explained that she had given up fighting and had surrendered to her enemy, PTSD. Once we surrender, we will be treated like a prisoner and humiliated by our enemy. We cannot expect our enemy to treat us gently and respectfully. If we want to get better, we must fight back. We must also accept the reality of the frightening event that caused the PTSD. Since the accident, unconsciously Sylvia had demanded of the world absolute assurance that she would be safe whenever she crossed the street or drove a car. Unfortunately, there are no guarantees of safety in life. Demanding safe passage only sentences us to be prisoners of PTSD forever. The accident had spooked Sylvia's emotions, and they now had a strong, irrational sway over her behavior, overriding her instincts. It is the role of the instincts—in cooperation with the intellect and the emotions—to evaluate threat to life and limb. Is the threat real or imaginary? Is it implied or imminent? The instincts know that surviving is about taking one calculated chance after another without distorting the truth. If Sylvia wanted to enjoy her freedom once again, I told her, she must put her instincts back at center stage in her mind. She must also accept the fact that she would always be particularly cautious when crossing a street or driving her car.

Sylvia received four Turning Point Treatments over the course of three months, and the stranglehold of PTSD began to loosen. First, I worked to calm her emotions. Then I encouraged her to face her problem with courage, think about it clearly, act confidently, and take responsibility for her actions and their consequences. Sylvia's mellowed emotions began to trust her instincts to restore peace and sanity in her life. With her instincts in charge of her actions, she was able to take calculated chances instead of demanding absolute safety. She gradually started to drive when the traffic was light and began to take long strolls on the sidewalk. As the days passed, even crossing the streets got easier. Six months after she had first come to see me, Sylvia was feeling so good that she asked me if she could stop taking Xanax and Zoloft, and I was happy to help her taper off of the medications. One year later, she was able to drive everywhere and cross the streets with only slight trepidation.

In Sylvia's case, she was able to identify the traumatic event that had turned her life upside down, so it wasn't difficult for me to guide her properly. Treatment for PTSD is more complicated, however, for those with no recollection or only dim recollection of the traumatic events that are holding them hostage.

A CASE IN POINT: My patient Susan was thirty-nine years old and an active and bright individual. She came to seek my help for her fear of heights. She came from an affluent family and had married a wealthy businessman. Together they had two children, aged seven and five. Susan was happy with her life, except that she could not tolerate heights. Her husband and children liked outdoor sports, especially mountain hiking. She loved her family very much, and every time they went on vacation to a mountain resort, she felt sad when she had to stay back in the hotel while her family went hiking. Also, as a native New Yorker, she felt cheated because she hadn't been able to visit the Empire State Building. She wanted to beat the odds and get to the top of that building. She considered her intolerance of heights a handicap, and having such a handicap did not resonate well with her.

She had been racking her brain for a rational explanation for her fear. She could not accept that she was scared of heights for no good reason. She consulted internists; ears, nose, and throat specialists; and neurologists for possible answers, but the test results came back normal, and the doctors concluded that her problem was psychological. She was resistant to this diagnosis, but she eventually accepted it and sought help from a psychiatrist. He suggested biofeedback-assisted cognitive therapy. Susan was hooked to gadgets that displayed the rhythm of her heart, her heart rate, and her blood pressure, all indicators of the stress response. She watched the changes in her vital signs while the therapist walked her through a simulated situation, for example imagining looking down from a mountain peak. The therapist then prompted her to consciously bring her vitals to normal levels. After a few practice sessions, Susan was supposed to be able to face the actual situation without fear, but even after fifteen sessions, when she tried to stand on a second-floor balcony, she felt as dizzy and light-headed as before. She was utterly disappointed.

Throughout our initial conversation, I observed that Susan used the word "scared" only once. Instead, she said she "could not tolerate" heights. When I pointed out this word choice to her, she confessed that she didn't like to think of herself as a "scaredy cat." When I questioned her further, she said she couldn't recall any accidents she'd had involving heights. As far as she could remember, her discomfort came out of nowhere one day when she was in seventh grade when she stepped out onto a third-floor balcony and felt light-headed and dizzy. These sensations became severe when she tried to bend down to talk to one of her friends on the ground. She pulled back immediately and sat on the floor until she recovered from the spell. From then on, every time she looked down from a height of more than ten feet, she felt as if she were looking down into an abyss that was about to suck her in. She would experience heart palpitations and feel as if the blood had been drained out of her brain. Ultimately she feared that she would lose consciousness, fall, and seriously injure herself. At the end of our initial consultation, I was at a loss to explain her fear in rational terms.

My hypothesis was that she was suffering from PTSD, but I couldn't be sure. I thought that Turning Point Treatments might reveal the mysterious trauma behind the conditions, but I do not like to offer treatments without explaining clearly to the patient the problem and my strategy for solving it. I explained my dilemma to Susan. She wanted to try the treatments anyway, and in the end she convinced me to give her a couple. Halfway through the first session, Susan appeared to become frightened. She began to cry and call for her mother. She wanted her mother to come and get her, to pick her up. I tried to calm her down and make some sense out of her words, but I failed. I terminated the session, realizing that Susan must have experienced some kind of trauma when she was young, something she had no recollection of as an adult.

Luckily for us, Susan's mother had accompanied her to my office. When I told her what had happened, she recalled that when Susan was three years old, she had wandered off and fallen down into their empty swimming pool, which was being repaired. Naturally, Susan was frightened and cried out for her mother, who came and pulled her out of the pool. Susan was not hurt badly, as the pool was only four and a half feet deep, and her mother had never mentioned it to her, thinking it a minor accident. The event, however, had been quite traumatic for Susan and was etched deeply in her emotions. Naturally, it manifested itself in a fear of heights. Susan was relieved to finally uncover the truth about her fear.

In spite of the best efforts of even careful parents, children will experience childhood traumas, the emotional reverberations of which children do not have the understanding or the language to communicate. Like it or not, they will unknowingly carry the baggage of these traumas for the rest of their lives. In young children, before the development of narrative memory and a mature intellect, a frightening experience is registered in the unconscious part of the emotions without the actual physical details of the event itself. Many times such memories will remain dormant without any repercussion on the overall behavior of an individual. However, in Susan's case, a specific event—the act of looking down from a third-floor balcony—bore some similarity to her childhood trauma, and the current event activated the buried memory of her frightening experience. Once the memory was triggered, PTSD set in, causing her fear of heights.

When people who suffer from PTSD are able to identify the source of the condition, then it is relatively easy to defeat it. However, when the victims cannot pinpoint the source, they cannot give up the fight but must instead address the negative impact of PTSD. Whether or not the source has been revealed, the following guidelines (which helped Susan) may be beneficial in defeating PTSD:

1. PTSD is not an invincible enemy. Therefore you have a fighting chance to defeat it.
2. Stop looking for a magic pill or an easy solution.
3. Utilize all your resources (family, friends, a therapist, research on PTSD, and so on) to identify the source of your PTSD.
4. If you wish to live a normal stress-free life, then refuse to be incapacitated by PTSD.
5. Finally, learn to distinguish between an implied threat and an imminent threat. For example, Susan can eliminate the imminent threat of falling and injuring herself by being vigilant and taking appropriate safety precautions. However, she cannot eliminate the implied threat that is associated with heights. Therefore, she must accept the possibility of getting hurt whenever she steps onto a balcony or crosses a bridge.

Once a person accepts the risks and is willing to be vigilant and cautious, he can defeat PTSD.

Susan liked my explanation and my proposed solution to her problem. She promised to follow my advice and was eager to seek closure on her past traumatic event and move on with her life without further assistance from the Turning Point Treatments. Eight weeks after her last visit, I got a call from her. She said she was on top of the world, literally, explaining that she was calling from the observation deck of the Empire State Building and feeling great.

Sometimes an individual is mature enough to understand and recognize a traumatic event but fails to connect the emotional impact of that event to the PTSD from which they suffer later in life. We must recognize all the pertinent facts and connect the dots to see the picture clearly. If we miss one detail, we might fail in our endeavor to defeat PTSD.

A CASE IN POINT: Eleanor was a fifty-two-year-old woman who sought my help losing ninety-five pounds. She weighed 225 pounds on our scale, and for her height and age, her optimal weight to look good and feel energetic and healthy was 165. Eleanor understood that the way to lose weight was to eat less and exercise more, but when she tried to implement this seemingly simple formula, she only ended up gaining more weight.

I asked Eleanor why she wanted to lose weight and why she thought she had failed in the past. Her health was the first reason she gave me for wanting to lose weight. Every day her aching joints reminded her how being overweight hurt her health. Yet she continued to eat more than she needed and gain more weight. Her weight was also affecting her love life. She had married her husband, John, when she was forty-five. It was her first marriage and his third. She loved him very much and wanted to make him happy in bed. She had tried all kinds of diets, medications, and therapists, but every time she made some progress and lost fifteen to twenty pounds, she would become restless and anxious and these emotions would spur her to go on an eating spree. She would not stop until she had gained all the weight back and more. She didn't understand why she was intentionally sabotaging her attempts to lose weight and look good, but she had decided that if her work with me failed, she would opt for what she thought of as her last resort—bariatric surgery.

I wanted to know in detail about her travails with her weight and how they were related to her sexuality. She told me that she had always been a big-boned person, but until she was a teenager, she maintained a healthy weight and stayed physically active. When she was fourteen, many of her friends became sexually active, but Eleanor was not interested in sex. Whenever boys made sexual overtures toward her, she felt uncomfortable. She stayed away from them whenever she could. It was around that time, she said, that she'd started to eat more and gain a lot of weight. Since then she had never had a healthy relationship with food or her sexuality. She told me that while she was in college, she had tried to have sex with a boy she loved, but she was not enthusiastic about sex because she never attained orgasm. Because of her weak sex drive, she had waited a long time to marry.

My interpretation of the situation was that Eleanor was using her weight as a shield against sexual advances by men. I knew that there was more to her weight problems than met the eye. I told her that she was holding back something from her past from me. I told her that I could not help her if she was not honest and forthcoming with me. With tears in her eyes, she reluctantly confessed that she had been sexually molested at the age of ten by a trusted individual. All the years since then, she had kept this horrible event bottled in her heart. She was ashamed to even talk about it.

I asked Eleanor if she really loved her husband and her body. She said yes to both questions. Looking deep into her eyes, I told her not to hold her husband and her body hostage to a despicable act perpetrated by a vicious sexual predator. I told her, "In fact, he should be ashamed of his act, not you. You were an innocent victim of a heinous act and should not punish yourself. If you really want to punish him for what he has done to you, you will move past the incident and lead a normal life with your husband. That's how you take revenge on the beast. I know you are angry at him for what he did to you and that he escaped scot-free. Don't be angry. I honestly believe that in the grand scheme of things, justice will always prevail. The person who betrayed your trust and took advantage of you will be held accountable for his actions by Our Maker."

Eleanor decided to leave her past behind and open up a new chapter in her life. I gave her two Turning Point Treatments, and a year later she was happy to report that she had lost thirty pounds and was enjoying every second of intimacy with her husband. As soon as she lost more than twenty pounds, she knew that she had broken the spell of the dreadful, traumatic event of her past.

Sexual molestation of an innocent and trusting child is the most heinous crime there is. Physically, the child may grow up to be healthy. Emotionally, the child is scarred forever. Victims of sexual molestation suffer from low self-esteem, lack of confidence, guilt, and rage throughout their adult lives. They feel they're second-class citizens in society. They experience intimacy problems because of inhibited or inadequate sex drive. Gripped by guilt and anger, many victims struggle to lead normal lives. My message to all victims of sex crimes is this: You did nothing wrong, so let go of your guilt, and stop punishing yourself. It is all right if you harbor some resentment toward the person who hurt you and the people who failed to protect you. It is all right to remain suspicious of other people's motives. But you will only punish the perpetrator by turning your life around for the better and leading a peaceful, productive life.

As we've seen, PTSD can result from severe trauma, as occurs during war, or from what seems to the outside world a minor childhood incident or fender-bender, but either way, it is no joke. The intensity and characteristics of PTSD depend on many variables, such as the disposition of the individual and the nature of the trauma. However, once PTSD makes its entrance, it will stay until its host kicks it out like an unwelcome guest. The longer the mind allows it to stay, the harder it is to erase PTSD from your life. Therefore, it is imperative to take swift action against it.

A CASE IN POINT: In the winter of 1986, my family and I decided to visit my sister, who lived sixty miles away from us. The weather forecast was clear and sunny, so we left in the morning and got on the Taconic Parkway heading north, planning to reach her place within ninety minutes. Halfway through the trip, snowflakes began to fall. I was driving, and I became concerned because at the time we did not have an all-wheel-drive vehicle. Even if I wanted to turn back toward home, I would have to go another three miles north on the parkway to make a U-turn. I decided to try to make it to my sister's place before the weather turned ugly. After another ten minutes, we encountered heavy snowfall, making it quite difficult to drive. While I was negotiating a downhill curve, I applied the brakes, and my car began to spin. The next thing I knew, my car was skidding sideways across the parkway, hitting the guardrail first on one side and then on the other. I froze behind the wheel. My car continued to turn 180 degrees before coming to a standstill facing oncoming traffic.

I was in a panic, but somehow I forced myself to come to my senses enough to take action to protect my family. The engine was still running, and with some difficulty I was able to turn the car around and drive in the right direction again. I drove to the next exit, which was about two miles away, and parked the car in a safe place. My family members and I were all shaken up but relieved that no one had been injured.

I stepped outside to inspect the car for damage. The sides and the front were pretty banged up, but the car was in a drivable condition. I drove at a snail's pace for the next twenty miles until we reached my sister's place. I was exhausted but relieved. We shared our ordeal with my sister and her family. The next day we returned home without incident, I got my car fixed, and I thought nothing more of it.

The next time we went to visit my sister, in the summer of 1987, however, I chose a different route instead of the Taconic Parkway, even though it is the shortest route to her house. It is also a beautiful scenic parkway on which no commercial traffic is allowed. But I had been avoiding it since the incident the previous winter—the incident had spooked me. I did not like that feeling and decided to break the spell. The next time I needed to travel that way, in the fall, I intentionally tried to take the Taconic Parkway. But at the last minute, I changed my mind and took an alternate route.

Usually, I love to drive on the parkway in the fall to see the bright foliage on the trees, a breathtaking sight. When I tried to force myself to take the parkway for my next two trips and again backed off at the last minute, I realized that PTSD had gained a foothold in my mind. I decided to nip it in the bud, knowing that, unchecked, PTSD would continue to expand my fears and inhibit my actions until I would not only have trouble driving on the Taconic Parkway but also on other highways. I adopted the slogan "When the going gets tough, the tough get going," for my battle.

First, I decided that I would face my enemy with courage on its turf. I chose a beautiful, sunny fall day to drive on the parkway. With clarity, I planned a route that would take me past the spot that had spooked me. On the appointed day, I got into the car alone. I shifted into drive and set out for the parkway, confident that I could meet the source of my stress head-on and conquer it. When I came to the spot where my car had skidded, I was a bit nervous, but I passed it without a hitch. I felt great relief. I came back home feeling like a conqueror.

In order to cure PTSD, its victims first need time to recover from the trauma in a safe environment. What makes it so difficult for some of our military personnel to overcome their PTSD is the fact that they don't have time to recover from one trauma before they are deployed again. According to one study, US troops have a higher rate of PTSD than British soldiers.[3] This contrast may be due to the fact that our troops are deployed for longer periods and have shorter time back home between deployments. American soldiers are also deployed more frequently to "hot zones." Active soldiers with PTSD need time at home combined with vigorous mental health treatment if we are to expect them to be fully functional soldiers or even normal human beings.

For all of us, but for soldiers especially, PTSD often carries a stigma of weakness. It is crucial for those who suffer from PTSD to acknowledge it without shame, since that is what allows us to stand up to it and fight back. It is also important to understand that PTSD occurs because the emotions have overpowered the instincts and the intellect, and that these three aspects of the mind must be balanced once again for PTSD to be conquered. A sound philosophical outlook in line with the laws of Nature, along with a good support system made up of family and friends, is an invaluable tool in fighting PTSD. Psychotherapy and group therapy can also be of immense help. And as we've seen, my Turning Point Treatments are also a powerful weapon against PTSD. Medications of any kind, however, are of little help in overcoming the condition.

*Conclusion*

# Naturization

## NATURIZING YOUR MIND

*Naturization* is a philosophical concept I have coined to reflect the intricate relationship between human beings and Nature when people live in accordance with Nature's laws. The cornerstone of my Turning Point Program, naturization starts with acknowledging that Our Maker created this world and ends with our agreement to abide by its rules. Naturized people develop a sixth sense, the attainment of which marks the turning point of their lives. This sixth sense offers a three-dimensional view of the world. The first dimension is Natures' point of view; the second is your personal point of view; and the third is the world's point of view. Naturizing gives you the power to conquer stress, and while it will not make all your problems disappear, it will put you in the best frame of mind to take on any challenge that unfolds in your life and do the best you can do within your limitations. It is indeed the only method that guarantees a stress-free life, a life of peace and productivity.

The laws of Nature are written in stone, and as we've seen, attempting to manipulate them to our liking is an exercise in futility. Often the undisciplined emotional mind, the aspect concerned with the self and its wants, will try to lead the instincts and the intellect on a path other than the one Nature has defined. When you naturize your mind, you encourage a balance between the three aspects of the mind, with the instinctual mind playing a prominent role. Nature speaks first to our instincts, the oldest part of our minds. Naturizing our minds means training the emotions to work in harmony with the other aspects of the mind. Naturization ensures that we check in with our instincts first rather than our emotions. This means that while the emotions continue to be the policy makers, they seek the input of the instincts and the rational views of the intellect when deciding how to behave. Naturization can transform a selfish, brash, overconfident individual ruled by emotion into a sensible individual who thinks first and acts later.

Naturization humbles us without hobbling us. It enlightens us to the fact that while our best bet is to toe the line with Nature, we are still masters of our own destiny. When we are humbled, our balanced instincts, intellect, and emotions allow us to solve problems with courage, determine goals with clarity, and act with confidence. We know naturized individuals when we see them, for they stand out in a crowd. In the world of high finance, Warren Buffet of Berkshire Hathaway has perfected the strategy of buying low and selling high. He has done so, arguably, by letting his instincts and intellect dictate his decisions while his emotions play a supporting role. He has made billions upon billions of dollars; yet he is not in his profession simply for the money but because he enjoys what he does and is good at it. His care for others is apparent in the way he treats his clients and their investments. His intention to make the world a better place is apparent in his generous philanthropy. In contrast, financier Bernard Madoff let raw emotions—selfishness, greed, pride, and deceit—dictate his decisions. He not only hurt himself but also his family and the clients who trusted him.

As a naturized individual, I consider my life on this earth an assignment given to me by Nature, one that I will complete to the best of my abilities in an honorable way. Working in concert with the laws of Nature has helped me define my role in life, determine my responsibilities, and discharge my duties accordingly. For example, whenever I am about to administer anesthesia to a sick patient in the operating room, naturization has conditioned me to let my instincts and intellect, supported but not ruled by my emotions, serve the needs of the patient and ensure a positive outcome. My strategy has served me and my patients well all these years.

How do you make naturization an integral part of your life? A novice may find it tricky at first, but just like riding a bicycle, once you've learned, the skill becomes automatic. As in the process of learning to ride a bike, you may fall a few times before you get the hang of following Nature's mandates and balancing instinct, intellect, and emotions accordingly. And like learning to ride a bike, the speed with which you learn naturization depends on your motivation. If a child wants to fulfill the dream of joyriding with her friends, she will master the technique of riding a bike quickly. Likewise, if you are determined to experience prosperity and peace of mind in your life, you will quickly surmount the initial hurdles, take your missteps in stride, and enjoy the benefits of naturization for rest of your life.

No two human beings are alike in their traits, experience, or sources of stress, so naturization will be different for each individual. However, the following guidelines are meant to help you to work closely with Nature:

1. Commence the process of naturization by respecting Nature and its creations.
2. Believe in the enormous benefits of naturization.
3. Show your desire to naturize through action, by naturizing with every step as you walk through life.
4. Understand what is relevant to your life from Nature's point of view, and then act from your instincts with input from your emotions and intellect.

## NATURIZATION: PERSONAL AND POLITICAL

Nature dictates that the mind needs a clean brain and a healthy body to be sharp and swift. Therefore, avoid unnecessary chemical agents and prescription and nonprescription drugs. Be active and eat healthily. I rely on natural foods such as vegetables, grains, legumes, fruits, nuts, milk, and eggs, which provide all the necessary nutrients that my body needs. I recommend that you get 75 percent of your nutrition from plant-based sources and 25 percent from animal-based sources and minimize or eliminate processed or packaged foods.

Nature also dictates that there are many things out of our control in this world. We cannot expect to ever feel completely safe in this life. We cannot predict our future or read another person's mind, but if we're smart and savvy, we can neutralize imminent threats. We will never, however, escape implied threats, and to try goes against Nature's laws. Yet, rather than let go of what we cannot control, Americans express their fear and uncertainty in government and economic policy, allowing the emotions to lead. The events of September 11, 2001, ended the American illusion of safety on home soil. In the aftermath of the attacks, the erratic and emotional response of American leaders only made matters worse. After spending billions of dollars and losing the lives of thousands of dedicated servicemen and women, years later we have yet to vanquish the threat and safeguard our security. Are we safer now that Osama Bin Laden has been eliminated? No, because the implied threat of terrorist attacks cannot be eliminated, ever.

If the United States were a naturized culture and American leaders assessed national security as naturized individuals, they would realize that the enemy is not a ruthless dictator or a country or even a group of terrorists. The enemy is religious idealism in the hands of clever individuals who use it to persuade their followers that the poverty and hardship they experience every day is the fault of Americans, whose very existence is an insult to God. This is an open-ended threat. Afghanistan and its neighbors will remain the breeding ground for intolerance to non-Islamic religions, vengeance, violence, human rights abuses, and shattered hopes for a better future. Until the people of these countries revolt against the ideals that define them and are willing to improve their economic conditions and raise the standards of living, our safety will continue to be threatened. Rather than wage an impossible war on terror, we must focus on protecting ourselves within our own borders.

As we've established, it is simply a hard fact of life that threats to our well-being exist at every turn. If we respond to these threats with paranoia, we are destined to spend the rest of our days stockpiling canned goods and weapons. Paranoia is an illogical response to an implied threat, a decision to allow the emotions to rule not only the mind but the behavior. Vigilance, on the other hand, is the response of the naturized mind, which speaks first to Nature through the instincts and then communicates with the intellect and the emotions to craft a strategy for protecting the self. Vigilance dictates that we watch for suspicious activity wherever we are, whether in an airport or a train station or walking on a city street at night. Vigilance does not differentiate between national security and personal security. It does, however, differentiate between implied and imminent threats. It relies on the instincts and the intellect to assess suspicious circumstances as they exist in the present moment, not as the emotions interpret them based on hearsay, prejudice, or fearful associations.

As individuals, there are ways we can address the issue of security at a national level—not because we feel stressed by the issue, but because we want to make the world a better, safer place, one less influenced by irrational stress responses. We can first talk with our family members, friends, and neighbors about adjusting paranoid and reactionary viewpoints. We can also communicate with our government representatives and urge them to address international conflicts with diplomatic measures. We can encourage them to research, develop, and adopt rational security policies, perhaps based on and adapted from effective policies in other cultures.

Economic hardship has become another powerful source of widespread stress over the past several years. Millions of people are unemployed. Families are struggling to meet their basic needs. The richest country in the world has been brought to its knees by irresponsible, cocky behavior from Wall Street to Main Street. Our present woes were in the making for many years, and it will take concerted effort on both an individual level and a collective level to turn our economy around. Even then, the recovery is guaranteed to take years.

The habits and attitudes that got us into this mess must be replaced by those of the naturized individual. First, we must stop spending money we don't have, both on the personal level and on the national level. When we want something we can't afford, we either have to go without it or save money until we have enough to pay for it. We must also stop buying big-ticket items, such as houses and cars, that we can't afford. If we look at our income honestly, we know what kinds of monthly payments we can afford to take on. When the economy was burgeoning, people in droves signed mortgage contracts they could not afford, urged by shortsighted, greedy lending institutions. Wall Street allowed substandard contracts such as mortgage-backed securities and structured investment vehicles to be traded without any consideration that they were building a house of cards. Federal regulatory agencies, such as the Securities and Exchange Commission and the Federal Reserve Bank, let our nation down by overlooking the long-term impact of these fast-track money-grabbing schemes. Everyone involved in this mess, from the home buyer to the federal regulator, has now been forced to take responsibility for the consequences.

As individuals, we can deal with economic stress the way we deal with any other stress. When naturized, we don't feel stress, only the ability to face any economic problems that may arise with courage, clarity, and confidence, according to the laws of Nature. Employed or not, the naturized individual will keep track of trends in the field and take any opportunity to upgrade professional skills, understanding that the world around us is always changing and can't be expected to do us any favors. Opportunities do not come knocking on our doors; we knock on opportunity's door.

To address economic security at a national level, we must insist that American employers stop outsourcing blue-collar and white-collar jobs to less-developed countries. Every time we outsource a job, we lose revenue and our competitive edge in the world. Labor unions must work with employers to cut costs and save jobs. America has the resources, technology, knowledge, and political freedom to pull itself out of economic troubles to become a financial world leader once again.

Another source of great national stress is the US health care system, which is arguably second to none in quality. The problem is that rising health care costs threaten to bankrupt us as a nation. If we are serious about offering quality health care for everyone at affordable prices, we must start the reforms from the individual consumer up the chain of command, all the way to the federal health care agencies.

Individual health care consumers have the greatest impact on lowering the astronomical health care costs in this country. For example, 40 percent of Americans are currently obese. Treatment of obesity-related health issues, including diabetes, heart problems, kidney disease, and joint failure, consumes billions of personal and government dollars each year. The sad fact is that these health problems are 100 percent preventable. In our culture we have turned our back on Nature and adopted the attitude that we deserve to be taken care of even when we refuse to take care of ourselves. This attitude must be exposed for what it is and individuals must be urged to take care of what Nature has given them.

On a national level, we must keep working to develop an effective, affordable health care system. Unfortunately, the present proposal passed by Congress to change the system will only make matters worse. It focuses mainly on disciplining HMOs, pharmaceutical companies, and other major health care service industries in order to cut health care costs. But these players are only partially responsible for runaway health care costs. Malpractice insurance and medical product liability issues are a huge drain of health care dollars, and these things are untouched by health care reforms. In an environment where household income is on the decline and insurance premiums, deductibles, and cost of medications are rising, none of us can afford to be sick. Count your blessings if you are healthy and protect this advantage however you can for the rest of your life.

## NATURIZATION VERSUS PRAYER AND MEDITATION

How is naturization different from prayer and meditation? Prayer is a religious tool, and meditation is a spiritual tool, but naturization is a philosophical tool. Religions recommend prayer for communicating with God. They characterize God as a loving, caring, compassionate, forgiving supernatural entity, who listens to humans and sometimes even grants wishes when they are in line with his divine plans. People pray to God for answers to their questions and solutions to their problems. Unfortunately, the real answers and solutions rest inside the individual and not with God.

Meditation is not bound by religious beliefs and consists of sitting quietly and clearing the mind of injuries from the past and worries about the future. It encourages people to practice experiencing the present moment. There are many recordings of guided meditations that aim to reach the unconscious part of the mind and work at the emotional level to change unhealthy beliefs about the self.

Prayer and meditation help their practitioners to relax, take a break from routine, and connect with what they interpret as a healing force. These practices do not, however, solve everyday problems. Sooner or later, we all must reenter the real world and find practical solutions to our problems. Naturization, more practical than either prayer or meditation, is not something we take time out of our busy day to do. It is a state of mind we practice twenty-four hours, seven days a week for the rest of our lives. When we have naturized our minds, the laws of Nature are the hallmark of our mind-set and the foundation of our thinking process every moment of the day, every day of our lives. Once you have mastered the art of naturization, you will see your life and this world from Nature's point of view. And in that viewpoint, you will find the answers to your questions and the solutions to your problems. Stress will no longer be of any concern to you, since you will have conquered it for good.

While I was putting the finishing touches on this book, I had an interesting conversation with one of my nephews. He is a well-educated, levelheaded individual. He disagreed with me when I argued that stress is inherently bad. Not all stress is bad, he told me. In his view there is good stress, and there is bad stress. For example, if he is working on a project, a little stress keeps him on his toes. The adrenaline generated by stress drives him to be in top form, he said. Similarly, a little stress encourages him to exercise and stay healthy. Without stress, he might become lazy and complacent and take his life for granted. Therefore, he would rather have a little good stress than no stress at all.

I disagreed with him. What he characterizes as good stress seems to me an imbalance between the instincts, the intellect, and the emotions. Rather than being motivated by the laws of Nature, which mandate that we take care of our bodies and always do our best, he seems motivated by emotions, namely fear and competitiveness. I, on the other hand, will not be driven by fear to maintain my edge in this world. I do not compete with this world. I compete with myself and do the best I can. My peace of mind is not a symptom of laziness or disconnection. On the contrary, it encourages me to be positively engaged in the world without fear or intimidation.

The differences between my nephew's argument and my own might simply be semantics. Perhaps he interprets the call of his instincts to be healthy and work hard as "good" stress. But I don't agree with an approach to life that highlights the negative rather than the positive.

Naturized individuals are driven by:

- A sense of elation when completing a task and hoping for the best possible results
- A sense of satisfaction in utilizing the talents and opportunities given to them by Nature and the world to create a peaceful and productive life
- A sense of accomplishment for making this world a better place
- A sense of acceptance that none of us gets everything we wish for in life
- A sense of gratitude for whatever Nature has given, whether that be health, talents, job skills, family, or friends

In the grand scheme of things, our lifespan on this earth amounts to a speck in time. Every moment of our lives is precious. Why waste it feeling stressed over things that are out of our control? Living stress-free means living for today and planning for a better tomorrow. It means striving to complete our daily tasks as challenges, not as chores. It means refusing to be miserable. Those who live stress-free are fighters. No one in the world can dampen the spirit that spurs us to protect our integrity, our freedom, and the values we cherish. We are at peace with ourselves and with this world, enjoying every moment of our lives.

# Notes

## Chapter 1: The Burden of Stress

1. Tamar Lewin, "Record Level of Stress Found in College Freshmen," *New York Times*, January 26, 2011. Retrieved from http://www.nytimes.com/2011/01/27/education/27colleges.html.

## Chapter 2: The Origins of Stress

1. Mayo Clinic Staff, "Single parent? Tips for raising a child alone," *Children's health at Mayoclinic.com*, June 22, 2011. Retrieved from http://www.mayoclinic.com/health/single-parent/MY01709.

## Chapter 5: Understanding Yourself and Your Place in the World

1. Jennifer Vargas, "Animals Just Want to Have Fun," *DiscoveryNews* (2011), http://dsc.discovery.com/news/2009/05/11/animal-pleasure-02.html.

## Chapter 6: Stress in Children

1. Melvin Lewis, *Child and Adolescent Psychiatry, A Comprehensive Textbook, Third Edition* (Lippincott William & Wilkins, 2002), 447–54.
2. *The March of the Penguins*, directed by Luc Jacquet (Burbank, CA: Warner Brothers, 2005).
3. Christine Armario, "1 in 4 American children raised by a single parent," *Children's health on msnbc.com*, April 27, 2011.

## Chapter 7: Post-Traumatic Stress Disorder

1. Timothy Williams, "US Soldier Kills 5 of his comrades in Iraq," *New York Times*, May 12, 2009.
2. James Dao, "Mental Health Problems Plague Returning Veterans," *New York Times*, July 17, 2009.
3. Benedict Carey, "U.S. Troops Suffer More Stress Than Britons, Study Says," *New York Times*, May 17, 2010.

# About the Authors

Balasa Prasad MD is a British-trained psychiatrist and an American-trained Board Certified anesthesiologist. He is the chairman of the anesthesia department at Mount Vernon Hospital, Mount Vernon, New York. He founded his behavior management clinic in 1980. Over the past three decades he has helped thousands of people free themselves from stress, addictions, and phobias through his innovative and highly effective Turning Point Program and Turning Point Treatments. He has been featured in the *New York Times*, *New York Post*, *Journal News*, *Elle Magazine*, and on TV on the *Inside Edition* news show. He is the author of *Stop Smoking For Good*, *Stop Gambling For Good*, and *Stop Overeating For Good*. He is the author of the e-book *Universal Sense: The Blueprint For Success*. For more information visit www.addictionandphobia.com and www.theturningpointprogram.com.

Preetham Grandhi MD is an Albert Einstein–trained, Board Certified adult psychiatrist, and Yale-trained child and adolescent psychiatrist. After his graduation from Yale, he has been the unit psychiatrist for House 5 at New York City Children's Center. He also has a child and adolescent private practice in Mount Vernon, New York. He is an assistant clinical professor in the Department of Psychiatry and Behavioral Sciences at Albert Einstein College of Medicine of Yeshiva University. He joined Dr. Prasad as an associate in the Behavior Management Clinic in the year 2000. He is the author of the award winning psychological thriller *A Circle of Souls*, which has received rave reviews from authors like Judge Judy and Linda Fairstein. For more information, visit www.acircleofsouls.com or www.preethamgrandhi.com

0 26575 10957 3